GOBBLE

THE QUINTESSENTIAL
THANKSGIVING PLAYBOOK

NADINE, PK & CHRISTOPHER ISACS

LOBA
PUBLISHING
Charleston, SC

Gobble

First Edition

Printed In China

ISBN: 978-1-95201-905-0

Dedication

This book is a love story. It is an expression of our love of food, wine, tradition, and most important, family. We write it in thanksgiving.

We dedicate this book to the memory of Peter, an incredibly loving husband and father who instilled in us an appreciation for all things good.

Table of Contents

Go to our website for a customizable Thanksgiving Checklist

We are
thankful for ...

...family inspiration.

Our small family of four has had the privilege of hosting Thanksgiving in our home in the Litchfield Hills of Connecticut for the past eighteen years. With extended family and friends, our gathering has been as small as twelve and as large as twenty-two. Our philosophy has always been the more the merrier.

How to use QR codes

If you are not familiar with QR codes, simply hold your smartphone or tablet camera over the code and it will automatically take you to the related content on the site. Alternatively, visit our website at www.TheGobbleBook.com

Looking back, we now realize that with each year we have raised the bar.

We have perfected the menu, elevated the table setting, and approached the planning and cleaning more efficiently. Most important, our joy and enthusiasm for the holiday has grown with each passing year.

The sudden death of Peter our husband/father in late August of 2020, combined with the restrictions of the Covid-19 pandemic, had the three of us bracing for an abbreviated and difficult holiday. One October evening after a glass of wine (or three), we were struck with the idea to write this book. Historically, in our family when one of us has had a good idea, we all tend to remember it as our own. We have since joked about which one of us actually initiated the idea for this book, but we now know in our hearts it was Peter. Throughout the process, we felt his spirit guide every strike of the keyboard.

Our intention with this book is to inspire both the expert and novice to continually raise their Thanksgiving game (pun intended), while at the same time making the execution easier, more efficient, and much more enjoyable. For this reason, we have called it a playbook, and have provided QR codes throughout that will direct you to complimentary videos, tools, and resources on our website. Our hope is to engage a community of Thanksgiving enthusiasts across the country, and maybe even across the globe.

A Note to the Host and Hostess

We recognize that Thanksgiving can be a production and sometimes can seem overwhelming. While we have tried to be comprehensive in our approach to this book, we encourage you to focus on what you love to do, and delegate or apply shortcuts to what you do not. Love cooking but not baking? Delegate or buy the desserts. Like the idea of a cocktail, but are concerned that they are labor intensive? Take a look at PK's batch recipes. Table settings not your thing? Copy one of the many on our website or purchase "a tablescape in a box." What's most important is to take the time to enjoy this special holiday. If that should mean a beautiful table setting and Kentucky Fried Chicken, so be it.

Allow Us to *Introduce Ourselves...*

Christopher

Nadine

PK

An Introduction to PK

by Nadine

When PK was entering the third grade, his teacher requested her class to prepare an "all about me" box into which each student would place their favorite items. PK chose to include the Zagat Guide—the annual book of restaurant reviews. It was fitting, as he'd kept a copy by his bedside ever since he could read. I kid you not. The only thing I think he liked as much as going to a restaurant was hosting or attending a party. The same is still true today.

When he was sixteen he designed a year like no other. He first spent six months living with a family in a remote city in China. They didn't speak a word of English. The remainder of the year he worked in Washington DC as a congressional page. He was my statesman and adventurer.

Before he was of legal age to drink, he developed an interest in wine, poring through the many books in our library reading about regions, varietals, and vinification techniques. Some of these books were handed down by his grandfather, and others were written by his uncle. His grandfather (Peter's father) was awarded the French Chevalier du Tastevin—an honor that recognizes only the top wine enthusiasts—and had established his own renowned cellar, referred to by Sotheby's

Wine as "one of the finest collections on the East Coast." Peter's brother, John, is a wine consultant to European trade offices in China, an author of several wine books, and is a weekly contributor on the subject for the Shanghai Daily newspaper. Clearly, it is in the blood.

It was no surprise that PK decided to attend Tulane University located in New Orleans, known for its culinary prowess, beverages, and parties. As you can imagine, all of that joie de vivre can be expensive for a college kid, so he earned extra money as a bartender. This supplemental education has served our Thanksgivings and other gatherings quite well. He is not only our very own certified sommelier but also our house mixologist, as he has a true knack for creating unforgettable cocktails.

An Introduction to Christopher
by Nadine

Until the age of 14, Christopher's diet consisted of hamburgers, chicken nuggets, steak, and ketchup. This changed when we decided to fly over to China to surprise PK for Christmas. During takeoff, Christopher declared to Peter and me, "I have decided that I am going to taste everything." As we all know, "everything" can be pretty adventurous when it comes to China. Much to our surprise, he did exactly as he'd said, dining on Chinese delicacies from duck tongue to fish eye. My picky eater was no longer.

Upon return, he took an active interest in cooking. He quickly became Peter's protégé, who had developed a reputation among friends and family as an accomplished cook. As PK had pored through the wine books, Chris pored through the cookbooks—and of those we have many. I believe one of the reasons he is so successful as a chef is that he balances the art and science of the craft by combining a deep understanding of the chemistry of food with an innate creative flair. His method is to read recipes but not to follow them, as he approaches cooking as a creative process. Again, it is in the blood.

Christopher visited PK in New Orleans, and as we should have expected, returned having decided to attend Tulane as well. I believe his exact words were, "Why would I go anywhere else?"

Many tell me that on campus Christopher developed a reputation for hosting elaborate, multiple-course dinner parties. By senior year, the invitation to one of his dinner parties was coveted.

They are coveted at home as well. My husband Peter had a very fortunate upbringing, dining at many Michelin-starred restaurants throughout the world. As a result, his standards were quite high. In my whole life—and we knew each other since I was ten—I never heard Peter say the common phrase, "This is the best thing I've ever tasted in my life," until last summer when Christopher had prepared a squash blossom stuffed with scallop mousse. By anyone's standards, this kid can cook.

Everyone who has been fortunate enough to taste Christopher's cooking has said at least once that he should open a restaurant. Chris politely tells us that he has no interest in doing so, as he is concerned that it would take the joy out of cooking for him. Instead, he is pursuing a career in software engineering, and intends to continue to refine and perfect his cooking skills on the side.

An Introduction to
Our Mom, Nadine
by PK and Christopher

Entertaining has been a large part of our lives ever since we can remember—from dinner parties with grand table settings in front of a roaring fire, to candlelit summer evenings under a pergola in our meadow, and just about everything in between. Over the years, our parents developed quite a reputation for being the quintessential host and hostess—Dad taking the helm in the kitchen and Mom creating the perfect atmosphere for festive and memorable gatherings. In fact, our parents' reputation so preceded them that they were sometimes asked to donate an evening soiree at our home for fundraisers.

It is not unusual to find guests taking photos of our mom's table settings. On holidays, friends would come to see how she had decorated to take ideas back to their own homes. It wasn't just that everything was in place—which it was—or that all of the colors and schemes matched so brilliantly. It was also the creativity that left people in awe. We remember one Asia-themed dinner party vividly from when we were quite young. She had set the table with a variety of plates, chopsticks, and rice bowls she and Dad had brought back from China long before we were born. In the center of the table, among what seemed like hundreds of small candles, were three fishbowls hosting one koi each, on short-term loan from our koi pond in the backyard.

"We are thankful for nights that turned into mornings,
friends who turned into family,
and dreams that turned into reality."

More important than table settings, Mom always made guests feel welcome.

Attending boarding schools close to our home, we often hosted international classmates who could not travel to their own homes for holidays. Mom would somehow get even the shyest of guests to open up and feel at home. She has a true knack for directing the conversation of the table without being overbearing. She always encourages others to speak without being direct, and guides the conversation to ensure that every person at the table feels included and has a memorable evening (especially our friends and us!)

Having taken on a bigger role in planning and executing parties at home, as well as hosting parties of our own, we still look to Mom as the prime example of how it should be done. We ask "What would Mom do?" and try our best to channel our inner "Dean," as we sometimes call her. And when that fails, we're thankful she's always just a phone call away.

We are
thankful for...
...traditions.

by Nadine

- **Popular Traditions**
- **Movies**
- **Games**

Families crave tradition during the holidays.

It provides memories of years long past and special moments that we might otherwise forget. Traditions are often handed down through generations. Sometimes they are deliberately created, and other times they are developed organically by repeating something from the previous holiday without even thinking about it. Some traditions are shared universally, and others are quirky ideas very specific to one family (pin-the-tail on the turkey, anyone?)

Why not start a new tradition this Thanksgiving?

We have gathered traditions that we think may be worthy of consideration if they are not already a part of your celebration.

We've gathered a list of trots on our website if you are so inspired.

Run or walk a turkey trot

Oh the agony of de feet! What a great way to build up an appetite and preempt the potential guilt of eating almost all of that pie by yourself. Here in Goshen, the 10k turkey trot has a 47-year history. While we don't participate every year, it is our tradition to say that we are going to participate, whether we actually do or not.

Have a ball

Channel the Kennedys and get the family outdoors for a quick game of flag football. *Why* flag, you ask? See the chapter on family dynamics…

Welcome weary travelers with a breakfast menu on their pillow

As I am certain many empty-nesters can relate to, I counted the days for the boys to return for the Thanksgiving holiday. Part of the welcome home tradition we adopted was to leave a menu on their pillows for their first breakfast at home. It included their childhood favorites such as "hard work pays off pancakes" (no boxed mix in these babies) and Mommy McMuffins, which you can probably guess are based on Egg McMuffins. While we knew the healthy option (yogurt parfaits) would never be selected, it was always included to make us feel better.

Start a tablecloth to capture memories

This past Thanksgiving, *The Today Show* featured a tradition where each family member writes on their tablecloth what they are thankful for. They use the same cloth year after year, continuing to add to it. Twenty years later, they have captured hundreds of entries. In my family, I can't imagine that there wouldn't be more than a few gravy and wine stains. Kudos to them!

Use a place card of gratitude and compliments

One host I know emails family and guests requesting each person to write one line of appreciation about each of the other guests. She then transcribes the compliments on a card that serves as a place card. Who doesn't love a few compliments?

Watch the Macy's Day Parade and the National Dog Show

In our kitchen, *The Macy's Day Parade* is a staple on Thanksgiving morning. As we are busily preparing for the day, there is no shortage of opinions on the performance, the performers, and what they are wearing. Directly following the parade is the dog show, where we wait for our favorite breeds—admittedly, they are sometimes hard to recognize. Our dearly departed Max, a Shih Tzu, bears little resemblance to his coiffed relative strutting his stuff for the show. We also love to be introduced to new breeds like Claire, the Scottish Deerhound who won in 2020. When will they include Golden Doodles and Cavapoos, we ask?

"What if today we were just grateful for everything?"

~Charlie Brown

Go for a post-dinner walk

Some years (depending on the weather) we will take a break between dinner and dessert and take a short walk. I remember one year it was snowing and we all donned our boots and walked down to the traffic circle (known locally as the rotary) in the center of our town. It was magical; big snowflakes fell against a backdrop of Christmas lights, and homes glowed from within, where we imagined families gathering by the fireplace. The brisk air can get everyone pumped for dessert, cleaning, game playing, a movie, or all of the above.

Prepare for getting the Christmas tree

It is our tradition to get our Christmas tree the day after Thanksgiving. We do this for several reasons. If we are going to go to all the trouble of putting up the trees (we have decorated two in recent years), we might as well enjoy them for as long as possible. Also, our guests are typically still with us, so we can take advantage of more hands to hang lights and ornaments. It's a great way to kick off the Christmas season. I just wish the guests were around after the new year to help take them down!

Host a friendsgiving

Friendsgiving parties are particularly popular with the young adult crowd. Before they were "in," I remember hosting and attending friendsgiving parties when Peter and I were considered yuppies (Young Urban Professional) and later DINKs (dual income, no kids) living it up in NYC. I'm dating myself, I know. Usually held just before Thanksgiving, a friendsgiving is an opportunity for eager hosts to throw a traditional Thanksgiving party that sharpens their entertaining skills while at the same time celebrating their friendships.

Watch a holiday movie or two

After finishing the Thanksgiving festivities, many families watch the same classic holiday movie that either marks Thanksgiving or kicks off Christmas. Every year our family watches *Love Actually*, which never seems to get old. If repeating the same movie year after year doesn't appeal to you, you could consider having each family member nominate a favorite and have the youngest or oldest select the movie from a jar.

While researching movies for the book, I was surprised how many of them were on the dark side. I personally don't do dark—particularly on Thanksgiving. For this reason, we have curated a list of feel-good movies that are short on tedious family drama and long on comedic family fun.

Families of all ages

A Charlie Brown Thanksgiving (animated)

Just thinking about this wonderful classic makes my blood pressure drop.

Premiering in 1965, this was the first TV special based on the comic strip *Peanuts* by the famous Charles M. Schulz. When I was a little girl, I remember waiting with anticipation for this to appear on one of our five channels. Today you can access it just about anywhere and anytime.

Elf

Elf may be my very favorite Christmas movie. It is a magical story that has all ages laughing. Will Ferrell, Bob Newhart, Ed Asner, James Caan, and Zooey Deschanel all give great performances in this now classic.

The Christmas Chronicles, 1 & 2

I've been a Kurt Russell fan ever since *The Computer Wore Tennis Shoes*, so it is no surprise I love him as Santa Claus. The original (2018), and *Christmas Chronicles 2* (2020) are both lighthearted and fun to watch. Goldie Hawn as Mrs. Claus in the second movie adds even more Christmas spirit to the franchise.

Families with preteens & older

Miracle on 34th Street

We all need to be reminded every once in a while that dreams do come true if you really believe, and this movie does that. Whether you choose to watch the 1947 classic starring Natalie Wood or the 1994 remake with hunky Dillon McDermott, it will not disappoint, and it's sure to get the whole family in the spirit! Just remember it could be a spoiler for little ones.

You've Got Mail

Yes…a chick flick, but Peter and the boys always enjoyed it. For me, it is one of those movies that stops my channel surfing in its tracks. Who can resist a Meg Ryan and Tom Hanks romance set in New York during the holidays? It is truly an enchanting movie.

Planes, Trains, and Automobiles

A favorite of many, this will keep the family laughing through the crazy antics of Steve Martin and John Candy as the two try to make it home for Thanksgiving through a freak snowstorm. This could be an especially good one if any of your guests have gathered their own share of horror stories traveling at this busiest time of the year.

It's a Wonderful Life

A black and white classic that reminds us that just being alive is cause for being thankful. Jimmy Stuart and Donna Reed show up on our screen almost every year as we revel in the story of an angel sent from Heaven to help a desperately frustrated businessman see what life would be like if he never existed.

Play a favorite game!

There are so many to choose from! Some require advanced planning (Pictionary) while others can be played on the spot (charades). Below is a list of some of our favorites.

The Name Game

Our family's favorite is what we call *The Name Game*. Since we cannot seem to remember the origin of the game, and it does not appear on the Internet, we will pretend that we were the geniuses who created it. We have had so much fun over the years playing this, and we urge you to try it. It doesn't require any materials and can be played anytime—even during dinner—with kids as young as eight (with a little help here and there).

Before explaining how to play, let me outline two important rules that will result in disqualification:

- Naming a person whose last name begins with the letter "H"—no Whitney Houston or Harry Hamlin
- Repeating a name that has already been said
- Making up a name (unless of course you get away with it)

Directions:

The first player (we choose the youngest) begins by stating a famous name. Let's say "John Wayne." The player next to him has to name another famous person, real or fictional, whose first name begins with the first letter of the last name, so in this case "W"—maybe Winston Churchill. Now, if the next player names someone whose first and last name both begin with the same letter, like Charlie Chaplin, the order reverses, flipping back to the previous player. This sometimes results in a back and forth dual. In our house, as the game continues and desperation sets in, you can expect that names will be made up and fact-checked.

The Family Game

Shortly after submitting the manuscript for this book, we were invited to a dinner by our dear family friends, the Owens. It was our first outing after being vaccinated. There were about fifteen of us between the ages of fourteen and eighty. After dinner they proposed that we play *The Family Game*, which we had never played before. On our ride home that evening the boys and I agreed that we absolutely needed to figure out a way to include the game in the book, as this game is guaranteed to bring disjointed families together and close families even closer.

Here is how to play:

- Each person writes the name of someone (real or fictional) that all family members know (famous or otherwise) on a piece of paper.
- One person collects all the names and reads them to the group, one by one. They repeat this step again (the names are read a total of two times).
- Everyone listens to the list of names, trying to remember as many names as they can.
- The first player begins by citing one of the names that was called and guesses who submitted that name. "Kitty, are you James Dean?"
- The player discloses whether or not he submitted that name. "No, I am not James Dean."
- If the guess is wrong, the next person selects a name and guesses who submitted the name. "Felix, are you Ruth Bader Ginsberg?"
- When a player guesses correctly, she acknowledges the correct guess, "Yes, I am Ruth Bader Ginsberg," and joins the "family" of the previous player that had guessed correctly. These players are now on a team and are rewarded for the correct guess with another opportunity to guess.
- Family members discreetly share the names they submitted so that they can better guess who submitted other names, and they work together to guess who is linked to each name.
- Eventually there are 2 or 3 large "families" that compete against each other for the remainder of the players.
- If a player correctly guesses the name submitted by someone who leads a family, the entire family joins the correct player.
- The last player who has not had their submission identified wins.

We are
thankful for...

...our beautiful surroundings.

by Nadine

- Table settings
- Buffet & Children's Tables
- Scents & Sounds

Let our lives be full of *thanks and giving.*

A stunning table sets the stage

for all that wonderful, decadent food and engaging conversation. For me, the ritual of setting the table officially launches the holiday. I usually take my time, beginning a few days in advance. This, of course, requires a night or two of family dinners eaten in the kitchen or family room.

My special love for table setting actually came from Peter's grandmother, whom we fondly called Grandma Glad. She was a woman of exquisite taste who lived in a beautiful house overlooking Long Island Sound in Black Rock, Connecticut. Her home was truly meant for entertaining. Peter's sister and I were best friends long before my lifelong romance began with Peter. When visiting her as a little girl, I was mesmerized by the festive tables Grandma Glad created. Satin tablecloths often laid the foundation for crisscrossed satin ribbons, mirrors, floral arrangements, crystal, and candlelight—it was like walking into a fairy tale! I think of her every time I set a table.

Step One:

Create the vision

Formal & Elegant?

Casual & Rustic?

Sleek & Modern?

What is your vision? Formal and elegant? Casual and Rustic? Sleek and Modern? Do you have special pieces or plates that you want to incorporate? Favorite china? The sky is the limit on where you can take your vision. You do, however, want to take the overall dining space into consideration. For example, a super modern tablescape in an old rustic barn may be difficult for even Martha to pull off. Then again…how fun would it be to set a formal table in a rustic barn with candelabras, silver, and fine china?

In addition to the photos in this book, look for *lots of inspiration* on our website and Instagram @thegobblebook.com

Step Two:

Determine your color scheme

T he traditional Thanksgiving color palate draws on the fall colors of nature, including oranges, reds, greens, yellows, and browns. Having said this, I have seen some creative hosts break tradition by creating stunning and festive tables of white and silver, blue and white, gray and black, and even turquoise and white.

I find the most cohesive tables focus on one or two foundation colors with a third color as an accent. Again, you will want to consider your surroundings. I once had a dining room with red damask wallpaper, which limited my options. What was I thinking? I have since remodeled it using neutral colors, which has greatly expanded the possibilities.

If your room or china is in a strong, non-traditional fall color or colors, think about using fall elements such as pumpkins and acorns for the table, and spray painting them in neutral colors like white, gold, or silver, then incorporating other natural elements like pine cones and moss. This will neutralize the strong colors while still recognizing the icons and traditions of Thanksgiving.

Some of my favorite color combinations for Thanksgiving are:

- Green and white with silver or mercury glass
- Blue and white with pops of orange
- Brown and green with gold tones

Step Three:
Select the backdrop for your first layer

Do you want the backdrop to be the surface of your table? Or, do you want to use a tablecloth, blanket, burlap, or even craft paper? Will you be using a table runner or placemats? Or maybe you'll run some beautiful ribbons down the length of your table. Perhaps you will use several table runners across the width of the table. There are so many ways to design your tablescape, it can be difficult to decide!

Step Four:

Select the anchor pieces for your second layer

Anchor pieces are the larger, sometimes functional pieces such as candles and candelabras, cornucopias, wreaths, flower vases, large pumpkins, silver or porcelain turkeys, etc. You may already have some of these in your basement or attic stash, or you could pick something up at the flea market or a local Home Goods store. I have also strolled through my house and given new life to things I pulled from a bookshelf—like an old trophy or urn that had previously been tasked as a bookend.

It is important to be conscious of scale. Mixing in a variety of sizes and heights will add interest, but be certain your pieces will not obstruct the view of people sitting at the table—unless, of course that's what you're aiming for! See chapter XIII on the dysfunctional family. My recommendation is to only select things for the table that you absolutely love. I must admit I have a number of things that never see the light of day (Thanksgiving or otherwise) because I did not screen them for love. Marshall's and I once had a thing, leaving me with a basement full of treasures I have been trying to unload for the last couple of years.

It is also important at this stage to think about function. While my personal preference is to serve the food on a buffet or sideboard, your tradition may be to serve the meal family style. If so, you will want to think about the space required, and imagine the food as your centerpiece. Think about incorporating cake stands or upside-down baskets or boxes that you can place the food on to vary height and add interest.

Old movies and Norman Rockwell art often portray the man of the house seated at the head of the table carving an enormous turkey prepared by the little woman. I'm not sure it works that way anymore. In fact, I'm not sure it ever did. I'm fascinated by the idea of anyone carving a turkey while sitting at the table—it seems uncomfortable for everyone! For this reason, Chris carves in the kitchen and arranges the delicious bounty on a beautiful serving platter to bring to the dining room.

Step Five:

Layer in elements of interest

In the spirit of abundance, my personal tendency is to go all out. I often lay down greens such as eucalyptus or magnolia leaves, and add fruits, artichokes, nuts, pine cones, or moss balls. Varying the textures and heights creates a beautiful and interesting tablescape.

A walk in your backyard or the woods can provide great inspiration. I look for bittersweet vine, fall leaves, moss, and evergreens. A trip to the grocery store can also provide an abundance of ideas.

From the produce section:

- Artichokes
- Pumpkins and gourds
- Pineapples
- Grapes
- Pomegranates
- Red and green apples
- Clementines or tangerines
- Pears
- Dried orange slices

From the floral section:

- Eucalyptus, magnolia leaves, and other greens
- White roses
- White lilies
- Orange lilies
- Orange tulips
- Sunflowers
- Succulents
- Moss
- Feathers
- Indian corn
- Acorns

Step Six:

Set the *table*

It is now time for the chargers (if you are using them) plates, napkins, silverware, and glassware. I sometimes like to place a decorative eight-inch plate on top of the dinner plate. Just before dinner when lighting the candles, I remove the smaller plates and reserve them for dessert. Over the years, I have invested in a few sets of affordable plates for this purpose.

Check the website for some of my favorites:

When placing the silverware, I always include the dessert spoon or fork, or both, so there is one less thing to think about when it's time for dessert.

Assuming a party of more than six people, it is important to place multiple salt and pepper shakers on the table so they are within easy reach of all guests. I like to place mini pairs of shakers between every two guests. There are plenty of attractive and affordable shakers for this purpose on our website and in stores.

Step Seven:

Add the finishing touches

I love using place cards. Not only do they help avoid confusion over where people are sitting, but they also add personality to the table. There are hundreds of fun ways you can present people with their names.

Here are just a few:

- Tiny frames with their name or photograph
- Paper tag tied to a pumpkin, baby artichoke, sprigs of rosemary, an acorn, or a pear
- Paper tag inserted into the shell of a walnut
- A baby white pumpkin with the name scrolled on it
- Small chocolate turkeys with a card inserted
- Paper tags tied to tiny wreaths made of rosemary
- Small chalkboards hung on the backs of the chairs with velvet ribbons that read *"I am thankful for... Name"*
- Tiny mason jars filled with cranberry sauce on each plate and the guest's name on the jar label

The basic place setting

The place setting of the silverware and plates can usually be simpler for Thanksgiving than a traditional formal place setting because most families do not have multiple courses.

If you are having multiple courses, the appetizer forks and knives are placed outside the main fork and knife. As a little girl I remembered this by thinking you eat from the outside in, so, like the glasses, place the utensils that will be used first on the outside.

If you are using a bread plate, that should be placed to the left of the main plate, above the fork.

A very basic setting includes:

1. Plate(s) in the center
2. Napkin to the left under the fork
3. Fork to the left
4. Knife to the right (blade facing inside)
5. Dessert spoon and forks at the top of plate (fork handle left, spoon handle right)
6. Water glass at the top right (an inch above the tip of the knife). If you are serving red, white, and sparkling wine (good for you, by the way!), set these glasses to the right of the water glass. Starting at the far right to facilitate pouring, position glasses in the order they will be used
7. If short on table space, wine glasses can be placed above the water glass, maintaining the white wine glass is on the far right
8. Red and/or sparkling wine is between the water and white wine
9. Sparkling glass is between the water and red wine

Feel free to get creative with napkin placement. Rather than holding it hostage under the fork you may want to place it on or under the plate, or in the water or wine glass. I have seen some hosts place the fork, knife, and napkin on the center of the plate tied with raffia or ribbon.

7

8

5

6

1

3

4

2

Step Eight:
The buffet table

Think of the buffet as an extension of your dining table.

Varying the height of the dishes and replicating some elements from the dining table will be alluring and erase any similarities to the dining halls of our youth.

Days before the holiday, Chris and I will select the various dishes and serving pieces we will use, and label them with post-its to remind us of the assignments. To help with cleanup, we try to select stove-to-table pieces if possible. Over the years, I have collected some beautiful casseroles, baking dishes, and pie plates, and have curated a small collection of yellowware. For me, the tradition of taking them off the high shelves from their eleven-month hibernation is a little like taking out the ornaments for the Christmas tree.

As for the gravy, we like to use pretty, pre-warmed pitchers instead of traditional gravy boats as there is less chance of spills, plus they keep the gravy hotter for longer.

Warm the platters

If you live in a cold climate as we do, I suggest you warm your platters. The most efficient way to do this is to place them in the oven after you take the turkey and side dishes out. Just remember to turn off the heat first!

Step Nine:

Set the dessert station

Many thanksgiving desserts can be decorative in their own right, so I sometimes display them—particularly the pies—on pretty cake stands in the dining room or kitchen.

How many can you fit at your table?

For comfortable seating, try to place chairs 24 to 30 inches apart.
Assuming we are not all still dealing with a pandemic, guests will understand
they may be sitting a little closer than usual on Thanksgiving in order to
accommodate a large group..

When your table is not big enough

It has always been important to me to have some flexibility with table size. In my first home, I had a French provincial table with leaves. But, there were times I just wanted to invite that one extra couple. For those occasions, our solution was to place an extra long plywood topper over the table and cover the whole table with a floor-length cloth. Similarly, in my second home I had a 60-inch round table that could only accommodate 8 to 10 comfortably. To extend this table, I had a large round topper made (with hinges so it could be folded and stored easily). For large dinner parties I pulled out the topper and again covered it with a floor-length tablecloth.

There are, however, inevitably times that numbers will require an additional table or two for overflow. In this case, I think it is important to make the secondary tables feel special. This may mean that one of the hosts or hostesses sit at the table. In jest, we have always called our secondary table Table #1. Be sure to give just as much attention to decorating the secondary tables as the main table.

Children's Tables

It has been our tradition to have the children eat with the adults. I know, however, that some families prefer to have a separate children's table. If this is the case, you can make it particularly fun by incorporating things that will keep the kids busy. Here are a few ideas:

- Use brown craft paper as your table cover and provide each place with a variety of crayons arranged in a small flowerpot

- Cut out paper turkeys as placemats and provide each place with a decorating kit (think glue stick, feathers, googly eyes)

- Place a jar in the middle of the table, full of kid-oriented questions. Each child picks from the jar and asks the question to the others at the table. Questions could be things like: What's your favorite cartoon character and why? What superpower would you most want to have? If you could only have one type of candy at Halloween what would it be?

We have gathered some fun templates on our website which you can download here

Warning!!

Beware of teenagers. The last thing you want to do is place a teenager at the children's table who believes they have outgrown it. Trust me, that teen is likely to hold it against you for life. Years later, you may wonder why she is always sick whenever you are in town, and why you are not invited to the wedding…

Seating arrangements

Be strategic with your seating. Traditionally, seating has been arranged in a boy-girl pattern. Of course, this is not always possible or even desirable. It is also tradition to place guests of honor next to the host or hostess. That may be appropriate for a new guest at your table. Also, consider that elderly guests may have a tough time hearing in a crowded room, or alternatively, may find a noisy dining room off-putting.

It's not just what you see, but also what you don't see

For the most part, wonderful aromas are already built into Thanksgiving with all the delicious cooking smells wafting from the kitchen. However, you may want to think about a fragrant candle or diffuser in the powder room, or in other areas that might be cut off from those wonderful smells. My favorite candle scent has always been pumpkin pie. I look forward to October every year so I can begin burning them, and happily continue all the way through Christmas. While scented candles are great strategically placed around your home, you do not want to use them in the dining room, as they will interfere with the mouthwatering aromas of the turkey and delightful side dishes.

Last but not least, music contributes significantly to a festive atmosphere, and it is so easy to orchestrate a good holiday score with today's technology. We think that Sonos speakers are one of the best inventions of this century. Combined with Spotify playlists, it is so easy to play the right music at the right time. We believe cocktail music should have a different vibe than dinner music, and certainly be different than cleaning music. For this reason, we have curated three different playlists of our favorites for the Thanksgiving Fête. Download them here:

We are
thankful for...

...Local Farms, Vineyards & Small Businesses

by Nadine

- Shopping Local
- D'Artagnan & the Farm to Table Movement

We feel so fortunate to live in the
Litchfield Hills of Connecticut!

THORNCREST FARM

We encourage you to visit this beautiful part of Connecticut.
If you are interested in sampling any of our local delicacies,
be sure to check out our website for more info.

I t is the home of many farms, vineyards, and specialty food shops. Our tiny town of Goshen alone (which doesn't even have a single traffic light) has one of the top vineyards in the state, a smoke house which Martha Stewart has been known to praise, and a chocolatier who customizes her cows' diet based on whether their milk will contribute to dark chocolate, milk chocolate, or white chocolate. The neighboring town of Bantam is home to the acclaimed **Arethusa Farm**.

The founders are the owners of the Manolo Blahnik shoe franchise. They started this dairy farm to create milk that tasted like it did when they were children. The results are the most decadent milks, ice creams, and award-winning cheeses. I wonder if it has anything to do with the fact that they use Pantene hair products to shampoo their cows?

Our intention each Thanksgiving is to use primarily local products. Our turkey is from **Bunnel Farm**, located a few minutes away. We shop for our produce at a fall festival the weekend before Thanksgiving at **Gresczyk Farms**. We make sure to include the Twisted Red from **Sunset Meadow Vineyard**, and our dessert table includes chocolate turkeys from **Milk House Chocolates**. All of our dairy products are purchased from Arethusa. Depending on the weather, we might also be able to harvest herbs from our own garden. We have found that sage, parsley, and thyme are safe bets even after a frost or two.

Litchfield is also home to **Litchfield Distillery,** where we purchase our spirits for many of the cocktails that kick off our very spirited holiday. Check out the Pilgrim's Reward cocktail in chapter V that their batchers co-created with PK.

D'Artagnan

If you or your neighbors are not turkey farmers, no worries, there is always D'Artagnan. If you are not familiar with D'Artagnan, run don't walk to their website *(you're welcome)*.

D'Artagnan led the farm-to-table movement. Long before terms like "sustainable" went viral, D'Artagnan has influenced how Americans eat meat. Founded over thirty years ago by Ariane Daguin, it is the go-to place for top chefs and novice foodies alike for the very best quality meats, poultry, *foie gras*, and charcuterie. They only sell non-factory-farmed animal products that have been raised conscientiously, ensuring the highest quality meat and poultry you can buy.

D'Artagnan has been a household name in our home for years. While writing this book, a friend put us in touch with Ariane, and she and her daughter invited us to their new farm in Goshen, New York (not to be confused with Goshen, Connecticut). For PK and Christopher, meeting Ariane was like me meeting Oprah. She did not disappoint.

In fact, she graciously invited Chris to her New York studio to shoot a cooking video.

You can easily order your turkey on D'Artagnan's website and know you will be getting a fresh, delicious bird that has been raised on a small family farm using the highest standards. While you're there, don't forget to order some mushrooms for the stuffing, and truffle butter for a variety of uses in the Thanksgiving meal and beyond.

We are
thankful for...

....Spirits & Cocktails

by PK

- The Basics: Tools of the Trade, Glassware and Menu Selections
- The Thanksgiving Bloody Mary Bar
- Mocktails, Pre-Batched, and Individual Cocktail Recipes
- Shrimp Cocktail and Herm's Cocktail Sauce

Cheers to a fabulous Thanksgiving!

As most Thanksgiving celebrations begin with cocktails, this is the opportunity to set the tone for the entire day. Before getting into ideas and recipes for libations, let's make certain we have the techniques down. Having worked at several New Orleans bars through college, I'll let you in on a few professional tips so you can sling drinks like a pro.

Maintaining the Bar

Whether you have a full bar setup with all the tools of the trade, or you consider the bar to be a bottle of wine on a counter, it should be viewed as a sacred space. Making sure it remains organized and clean is challenging, particularly as the day goes on. Keep a couple of dishtowels, a roll of paper towels, and some countertop spray nearby where you can reach it frequently. Try to recycle empties whenever possible. If using a juicer, clean it immediately. Letting the juice and pulp remain on the juicer will make it far more difficult to clean later. Cocktail shakers and jiggers typically only require a rinse with water between cocktails, as long as it is done immediately.

Types of drinks

Drinks are typically served neat, up, on the rocks, or over crushed ice. Thanksgiving doesn't exactly conjure images of mai tais and piña coladas, so we'll stick to the first three categories for now.

When a drink is served **neat**, it is served at room temperature.

An **up drink** is shaken or stirred with ice, and then strained. If you are shaking your drink, add your ingredients, fill your shaker about two thirds of the way up with ice, and shake for about thirty shakes. Note that one of the mistakes home bartenders make most often is not shaking enough. Once shaken, double strain into a chilled glass.

For a **stirred** cocktail, add your ingredients to a mixing glass or cocktail shaker, add ice, and stir for about 50 or 60 rotations. Then, double strain the drink into your chilled glass.

Finally, there are drinks served **on the rocks**. Rocks drinks can either be built in the glass or whipped in a shaker before being strained and poured over ice. To build a drink in the glass, add all flat ingredients, then ice, and then top off with any carbonated ingredients. To **whip** a cocktail, shake it with only a few ice cubes, then strain it out over your chilled glass with ice. Whipping works best for cocktails that need to be aerated or more fully incorporated.

The Right Glassware

While a solo cup will get the job done, the right glassware can actually make a cocktail taste better, and make it more fun to drink.

We'll start with the basics:

Highball:

A highball glass is perfect for any sort of mixed drink, including a gin and tonic, vodka collins (though a collins glass is technically taller), screwdriver, or whiskey and cola. You name it. This is the workhorse of the bar.

Coupe glass:

This one is the go-to. A glass originating in the 17th century that gained great traction throughout the prohibition era, it can be used for champagne or pretty much any cocktail that's served up. This glass comes in a variety of shapes and sizes. It spills much less than a martini glass, and has a wide, curved mouth, allowing for bubbles and aromas to make their way to the top.

Rocks glass:

A short, simple glass, this is used for the old fashioned and other strong drinks that are served on the rocks, in addition to drinks served neat.

Nick and Nora glass:

The Nick and Nora glass named for the famous *Thin Man* detective and his wife, is a small glass resembling a wine glass, but without the curvature at the top. These glasses are best used for strong drinks that are served up, like martinis and manhattans. While not a total necessity for the bar, these glasses provide style and are very functional. Additionally, their diminutive size allows for drinks to stay cold, and serves as a deterrent for overindulgence. These formerly very popular glasses had fallen out of fashion until fairly recently. They are now the up-and-coming glass in bars across the country.

Martini glass:

While martini glasses have a classic appeal, we personally feel they aren't terribly practical. Given the size and the shape of the glass, you would think they were designed by someone who likes a warm martini. It is also almost impossible to carry one without spilling.

Shot glass:

Just figured we'd put this here, no explanation needed…

While other glasses, including brandy snifters and shiraz glasses, can be great additions to your bar, the glasses listed to the side are our top recommendations.

All-purpose glass:

Having said all of this, while not as fun, you may want to opt for an all-purpose glass that will accommodate both wine and cocktails. A burgundy style glass with a round barrel is a good choice as it can accommodate ice when necessary, and is also appropriate for white wine.

We have also taken a liking to the **Bodega glass,** which can be very adaptable to both wine and cocktails. They come in three sizes: 17.25 oz, 12.5 oz, and 7.5 oz, and are usually stackable.

Check out our favorite glasses on our website.

Tools of the trade

A well-stocked bar requires some fun bar tools.
You don't need every single item here,
but they are helpful to raise your cocktail game.

Cocktail shaker:

Cocktail shakers are typically used when there is fruit juice in the drink. While rules are meant to be broken, this is a good guideline as you start to build your cocktail repertoire. Most bartenders prefer a Boston shaker, which consists of one large piece and one smaller piece (or a glass). This is easier to use, and requires less cleanup than a martini shaker. Build the drink in the smaller glass, add ice to the larger, join them together and shake. If you don't have a mixing glass, you can use the smaller part for any cocktail that calls for mixing.

Sieve strainer:

A fine mesh strainer that will get out impurities that the Hawthorne strainer misses. These impurities include bits of fruit and shards of ice. While not necessary for all cocktails, double straining gives drinks purity, both aesthetically and texturally.

Hawthorne strainer:

A strainer designed to fit onto the top of a cocktail shaker or mixing glass to strain the cocktail.

Mixing glass:

A large glass with a spout, the mixing glass is typically used for drinks needing to be stirred, such as martinis, manhattans, and negronis. They often are made from cut glass, making them a pretty addition to the bar.

Jigger:

A jigger is a double-sided, "flippable" container used to measure liquid amounts. A classic jigger has either one-and-a-half or two ounces on one side, and one or one-half ounce on the other. We recommend a taller jigger (they are more accurate) and, ideally, one with measurement lines.

Bar towel:

We like to use two bar towels at the bar, with back-ups within easy reach. One is for the surface on which we prepare the drinks, and the other is for keeping your hands clean and dry.

"I come from a family where gravy is considered a beverage."

~Erma Bombeck

Which Cocktails to Serve?
There are several considerations.

The Food:

Thanksgiving is the most food-centric holiday in the Western world. Between the turkey, the endless sides, and what seems like a dozen pies, a meal of epic proportions is the norm. For this reason, light cocktails are appropriate. Cocktails that contain ingredients that either increase your appetite or settle your stomach are advantageous as well.

The Weather:

Darker liquors like whiskey are associated with colder weather, and lighter liquors like gin with warmer weather. I've listed drinks that are great for warm weather areas (fear not, Floridians), while others are designed for our Connecticut fall.

The Guest Demographic:

Depending on the age of your guests, the night before Thanksgiving can be important to consider. With the return of college students and young transplants to their hometowns, there is a lot of reconnecting occurring on Wednesday night. There is so much reconnecting, in fact, that Thanksgiving Eve is the busiest bar night in America, even more so than Cinco de Mayo, St. Patrick's Day, and New Year's Eve! As you can image,

this could lead to some hangovers (present company excluded). Whether you're an advocate of the hair of the dog that bit you, or rehydration and abstinence, some cocktail ingredients will help to remedy a hangover.

We also don't want to forget our underage drinkers and non-drinkers. A special mocktail in a fancy glass with a fun garnish is sure to make you the favorite aunt or uncle. A mocktail for more sophisticated tastes for the adult non-drinkers will be appreciated as well.

Ease:

With all of the commotion occurring throughout Thanksgiving Day, having a cocktail that is easily scalable and that can be prepared at least partially in advance is important. While we sometimes enjoy a bit of a dramatic flair in our cocktails, mostly we take steps to make the more challenging cocktails easier, and the easy ones more impressive.

Theme:

I never like to rely heavily on a theme for my cocktails. Pushing drinks like cran-tinis, cran-aritas, and cran-hattans is not my style. I am, however a big advocate of bringing in holiday cheer with creative names. If you are making a cocktail of your own design, or following a recipe (in which case you can use a little creative license), Thanksgiving-themed names can add a festive touch.

Some of Our Thanksgiving Favorites

T he first rule of cocktails is the same as the first rule of wine and food: What you like best is the best for you. The same applies to your guests. What follows are recommendations based on what we think works well at Thanksgiving, but at the end of the day the choice of what to serve is yours and yours alone.

There are three strategies hosts can apply to the Thanksgiving bar.

Open Bar:

Leave out the booze, mixers, ice, and glasses, and let the guests make their own drinks.

Check out our textable drink menu templates on the Gobble website.

À La Carte Bar:

An assigned bartender armed with all the staples necessary for the classics takes orders and prepares drinks accordingly.

Featured Cocktail Bar:

Guests are texted a selection of a few specialty cocktails designed by the bartender ahead of time. This is our favorite approach because it allows us to focus our preparation so drinks can be served efficiently. One of the great things about this strategy is that you can text a menu to your guests in advance so they can place their orders before they arrive. This gives the bartender plenty of time to prepare, while ensuring that everyone has a drink on hand shortly after arrival.

The Bloody Mary Bar:

We can't remember its origins exactly. Perhaps it began when one of our cousins brought a gift of bottled Bloody Mary mix and a fifth of vodka to ensure their preferred elixir was available. Remembering this, the following year we elevated our game by blending our own tomatoes for the mix while making certain that various hot sauces were on hand. Years following, we added, adopted, and improved our offerings until we had the perfect kickoff for Turkey Day—*a full Bloody Mary bar.*

You may be thinking Bloody Marys don't seem very practical for Thanksgiving (after all, who wants a filling drink before the biggest meal of the year?). Not to worry, we've got this covered. Clarifying tomato juice retains the flavor of the tomatoes and the nutrients that help with hangovers, but the juice is quite light. The good news is, it is very easy to make as long as you start the process the evening before.

Clarified
tomato juice

Ingredients:

- Eight tomatoes
- 1 clove of garlic, peeled
- 1 quarter serrano chili, seeds and stem removed
- 1/8 medium red onion, roughly chopped
- Pinch of salt

Directions:

Put all ingredients in a blender and puree until smooth. Line a large bowl with a few layers of cheesecloth. Pour the mixture into the bowl. Tie the corners of the cheesecloth together with butcher twine. Suspend the cheesecloth over the bowl overnight. We hang it from our kitchen chandelier—I know, this sounds weird. If that is not an option, perhaps you can hang it from your kitchen faucet. In the morning, you will find that the clarified juice has slowly dripped out of the cheesecloth and into your bowl. Voila! Clarified tomato juice! Pour it into a pitcher and place in the fridge until ready to use.

Bloody Mary Bar Fixings

Go simple, or go crazy! *Here's a list of what we think is absolutely necessary, to what may seem over-the-top.*

The necessities:

- Lemon juice
- Worcestershire
- Tabasco
- Celery sticks
- Scallions
- Bacon
- Salt
- Pepper
- Ice
- Vodka

Fun add-ons:

- Additional liquors for bloody marias (tequila or mezcal) and red snappers (gin)
- Local or homemade hot sauces
- Lighter hot sauces like Franks or Red Devil
- Eccentric hot sauces made from ghost peppers or habaneros
- Lawry's salt (for the rim, or a sprinkle)
- Tajin
- Lime wedges
- Bacon or beef jerky
- Fresh peppers
- Beef consommé (for a bloody bull)
- Fresh horseradish

Setting up the bar

There are a few key considerations when setting up your Bloody Mary bar. Be certain to have a clear starting point and a clear ending point. Glasses first and garnishes last. You may want to salt the rims of a few of the glasses in advance. We like to use Lawrey's salt. Bloody Marys do make a mess, so have bar towels and paper towels on stand-by.

The following cocktails
(some original, others classic)
are some of our
Thanksgiving favorites...

Mocktails

Turkey Trotter

If your Thanksgiving table has a member who abstains from alcohol but would also like a less Sesame-street option, we have an answer for you. Ginger has natural healing properties, and any health nut who ran the turkey trot will appreciate a grown-up, medicinal cocktail. Don't worry, though—this isn't cough syrup. This Thanksgiving mocktail can stand up to the very greatest of sours.

Ingredients

- 1 oz lime juice
- 1 oz grapefruit juice
- 1.5 oz ginger syrup*
- 1 egg white

Directions:

Combine all ingredients in a cocktail shaker without ice. Shake vigorously. Add ice and shake again. Double strain into a coup glass and garnish with a sprig of rosemary.

Say Grace

Ingredients:

- 1 oz Grenadine
- 2 oz Orange Juice
- 5 oz Sprite

Directions:

Add orange juice and ice to a highball glass. Add sprite, and then use a bar spoon to float grenadine on the top.

*To make the ginger syrup, combine 1 cup of demerara sugar with 1 cup of water in a pot. Bring this to a boil. Cut the heat, and add slices of ginger. Let cool, then strain and save for up to one month in a refrigerator.

Pre-Batched Cocktails

I know, I know!

Pre-batched cocktails sound like cheating,

but they can make your life easier and ensure that drinks are ice cold and at the ready. Another benefit to pre-batching is that you can control the dilution. When cocktails are shaken or stirred, they melt some of the ice and are diluted. In a properly-made cocktail, this dilution is typically between 20 and 25%. Pre-batching allows you to take all of the guesswork out of dilution by precisely measuring the amount of water you add.

Some pre-batched cocktails to consider:

Classic Martini

While a martini doesn't necessarily scream, "Thanksgiving!" this classic drink deserves a spot on any cocktail menu. It does have some Thanksgiving specific advantages—it won't fill you up, it is sipped in small quantities (we hope), and die-hard martini enthusiasts will be satisfied. Finally, as mentioned, martinis are excellent when pre-batched, making them super easy to serve.

Ingredients

- 15 oz gin or vodka
- 3 oz vermouth
- 4 oz water
- 8 dashes orange bitters

Directions:

Clean a 750 ml. bottle (your typical wine bottle will do) with hot water and allow to cool. Using a funnel, add all ingredients to the bottle, cork it, and place into the freezer for at least 12 hours. Keeps for up to six months.

Vesper

The vesper is a James Bond original. True, he works for the British Secret Intelligence Service, but we can only assume that someone who spends so much time talking about food, wine, and cocktails must be regularly visiting his American friend Felix Lighter on the last Thursday of November.

Ingredients

- 12 oz gin
- 4 oz vodka
- 2 oz Cocchi Americano Aperetivo
- 4 oz water
- 8 dashes orange bitters (optional)

Directions:

Clean a 750 ml bottle (your typical wine bottle will do) with hot water and allow to cool. Using a funnel, add all ingredients to the bottle, cork it, and place into the freezer for at least 12 hours. Keeps for up to six months.

Ingredients

- 9 oz gin or vodka
- 9 oz dry vermouth
- 4 oz water

Directions:

Clean a 750 ml bottle (your typical wine bottle will do) with hot water and allow to cool. Using a funnel, add all ingredients to the bottle, cork it, and place into the freezer for at least 12 hours. Keeps for up to six months.

Ingredients

- 13.5 oz gin
- 3 oz dry vermouth
- 1.5 oz maraschino liquor
- 12 dashes orange bitters
- 4 oz water

Directions:

Clean a 750 ml bottle (your typical wine bottle will do) with hot water and allow to cool. Using a funnel, add ingredients to the bottle, cork it, and place into the freezer for 12 hours. Keeps for up to six months.

"Small cheer & great welcome makes a merry feast."

~William Shakespeare, *The Comedy of Errors*

Manhattan

The manhattan has been a Thanksgiving tradition in my family for years. When my brother and I first started to enjoy the world of cocktails, manhattans were one of our early favorites. Up in Connecticut, it makes an incredible digestif as the sun fades and we fall onto the couches, full and exhausted.

Ingredients

- 10 oz rye
- 10 oz sweet vermouth
- 10 dashes angostura bitters
- 4 oz water

Directions:

Clean a 750 mL bottle (your typical wine bottle will do) with hot water and allow to cool. Using a funnel, add all ingredients to the bottle, cork it, and place into the freezer for at least 12 hours. Keeps for up to six months.

Individual Cocktails

Mayflower Mojito

We know that the mojito doesn't exactly scream, "Thanksgiving!" at first glance either, but hear us out. It's a light, refreshing drink that is almost universally adored (at least by the people drinking them), and brings an air of levity to one of the heaviest holidays around. Additionally, if you make the mojitos strong at the beginning (in other words, light on soda) you have the opportunity to lengthen your drink over time. When you've had a third to a half of your drink, add some more soda, and repeat until it's too light. This gives you the opportunity to experience the drink at different dilutions, and will make sure your palate gets progressively less overwhelmed as you approach the main meal.

Ingredients

- 2 oz rum
- 1.5 tablespoons cane sugar
- 3 lime wedges (each 1/8 of a lime)
- 12 mint leaves, freshly picked
- Club soda

Directions:

Add 1 lime wedge and mint to the bottom of a cocktail shaker. Muddle very lightly. Add the other ingredients and muddle again, making sure to expel the juice from the lime. Add ice, and pour back and forth between the cocktail shaker and a high ball glass. Without straining, add the drink to the glass, add ice, and top with soda. Garnish with a mint sprig.

Plymouth Rock

When the Mayflower neared Plymouth Rock, they encountered a problem—they were low on ale. Why they were running low is unclear, but the fact that daily beer rations were a gallon per person may give us a hint. Regardless of the reason, Captain Jones realized he and his crew needed to get back to England. Concerned that they would not have enough roadies to get them all the way home, Jones dropped the Pilgrims off at the nearest spot he could find, namely Plymouth Rock. If we had been there, we could've recommended that they use the beer as a cocktail ingredient to save on supplies.

Ingredients

- 2 oz rye
- 1 oz aperol
- 1 oz amaro nonino
- 1 oz lemon
- 4 oz IPA beer

Directions:

Place the rye, aperol amaro, and lemon into a cocktail shaker and add three ice cubes. Whip, then double strain into a large glass with an ice square. Top with IPA.

Settler's Sour

This take on a whiskey sour combines everything we love about Thanksgiving—it will brace you from the cold while reminding you of the warmth of the occasion. Like many of the Thanksgiving dishes, it provides spice, richness, and a touch of sweet to round out your palate.

Ingredients

- 2 oz rye whiskey
- 1 oz grand marnier
- 1 oz cinnamon simple syrup*
- 1 oz grapefruit juice
- 1 egg white
- 2 dashes barrel-aged bitters
- ¾ oz red wine

Directions:

Add rye, grand marnier, cinnamon simple syrup, grapefruit juice, and egg white to a cocktail shaker without ice. Dry shake. Add bitters, three cubes of ice, and shake. Double strain over a rocks glass filled with ice. Slowly pour red wine over the back of a bar spoon to layer the wine on top.

*Cinnamon simple syrup: In a small saucepan combine 1 cup water, 1 cup sugar, and 2 medium-sized cinnamon sticks. Bring to a boil to dissolve the sugar, then remove from heat and let steep for 20 minutes before straining.

Moscow Mule

The moscow mule was one of the most popular, drinks of the 2000s and 2010s. The combination of vodka, ginger beer, lime, and mint is simple and refreshing. The ginger brings in a distinctly wintery vibe, while the vodka, lime, and mint keep it light. The key to this drink, and to its various interpretations (for example, feel free to substitute bourbon for vodka to make it a kentucky mule, mezcal for a mezcal mule, or cognac for a french mule) is homemade ginger beer. See our recipe for taking your next mule to soaring heights.

Ingredients

- 2 oz vodka
- 4 oz ginger beer
- 2 mint sprigs
- ¾ oz lime juice

Directions:

Add vodka and mint to a mule mug, muddle. Add lime juice. Add ice, and top with ginger beer. Garnish with mint sprig.

Ginger Beer *by Chris*

Serving your own house-fermented ginger beer can be a show-stopper. It's perfect for Thanksgiving because all the work is done far in advance, most of the cocktails you make with it are quick and easy (like mules), and it's delicious and unique.

Preparation:

Start by grating fresh ginger (including the skin) using the coarse side of a box grater. You should end up with roughly 10-12 oz of grated ginger. Meanwhile, in a small pot make simple syrup by combining equal parts sugar and water. Bring to a boil to dissolve the sugar, cut the heat, and let it cool to room temperature.

Ingredients

- grated ginger
- 8 oz lemon juice
- 12 oz simple syrup
- 6 g cream of tartar
- 1-2 g active dry yeast
- 40 oz water

Directions:

Combine ingredients in a mixing bowl, mix well, and funnel into a 2-liter soda bottle that has been thoroughly rinsed clean (make sure you are using a bottle intended for a carbonated drink, so the plastic will be able to withstand the pressure buildup that occurs during fermentation). Leave in a warm, dark place for 2-3 days, checking regularly. As the ginger beer ferments, it will produce a lot of gas that will build up in the bottle. Whenever the bottle becomes very firm, burp it by carefully twisting the cap slightly open to let gas escape. To be safe, I recommend burping the ginger beer at least twice a day.

After 2-3 days, strain the solids out of the ginger beer and funnel the liquid into smaller soda bottles that have been thoroughly rinsed clean. Leave the bottles in a warm, dark place for an hour or two until the buildup of gas has made them very firm. This is called a secondary fermentation, and it will help with the carbonation of your ginger beer. Transfer the bottles to the refrigerator to kill the fermentation. The ginger beer will be ready two hours after refrigeration, but I have found that it is best after being in the fridge for at least a few days.

The Pilgrims' Reward

*In preparation for this book,
we sat down with the founders of the Litchfield Distillery*

to create a Thanksgiving cocktail. Their motto, "the spirit of hard work," was a great inspiration for the pilgrim's reward. Thanksgiving done right requires a lot of work, and while Thanksgiving Day is its own reward, at the end of the night the hardworking adults deserve a special drink by the fire.

Ingredients

- 1 oz Litchfield Distillery vanilla bourbon
- 1 oz Litchfield rye whiskey
- 1 oz grand marnier
- 1 oz honey syrup
- 2 oz lemon juice
- 1 egg white

Directions:

Combine all ingredients and shake without ice. Add ice, shake, and double strain into a rocks glass with a large ice cube.

a word on hors d'oeuvres

When we think about hors d'oeuvres on Thanksgiving, the phrase "gild the lily" comes to mind. The actual phrase used in Shakespeare's play *King John* is "To gild refined gold, to paint the lily, to throw a perfume on the violet...is wasteful and ridiculous excess." We couldn't say it better ourselves. For this reason, the only pre-feast nibble we are including in this book is a classic shrimp cocktail with a little twist, thanks to PK's take on Herm's cocktail sauce.

Shrimp Cocktail

by Christopher

Shrimp cocktail is a perfect appetizer for Thanksgiving. It is both light and easy to make. Of course, you could buy frozen, already cooked shrimp, but in the spirit of raising the bar, we recommend cooking your own shrimp (fresh or frozen). You may also want to consider purchasing shrimp with shells on, and peeling them after you poach them, which will result in the most flavorful shrimp.

By gently poaching the shrimp in a lightly flavored broth and making sure you don't overcook them, you can serve a shrimp cocktail to which the store-bought version will pale in comparison (store-bought shrimp cocktail is almost always overcooked, rubbery, and lacking in flavor.)

Directions:

If the shrimp are frozen, thaw them by running them under cool water.

Bring a pot of water to a boil. Generously salt it like you would if you were making pasta. Cut a lemon in half, squeeze each half into the water, then throw in the husks (that way the water gets the flavor from the lemon peel as well as the flavor and acidity from the juice). Toss a few bay leaves into the water as well, and some black peppercorns if you'd like. Any flavors you impart in the water will have a subtle yet satisfying impact on the shrimp.

Reduce the heat to a low simmer and add in the shrimp. The time it takes for the shrimp to cook through depends on the size of the shrimp, but it won't take more than a minute or two (and may be even shorter).

You'll know the shrimp are ready when they turn pink, become a bit stiff, and their tails just start to curl in.

When the shrimp are cooked, remove them from the pot and immediately shock them in a bowl of ice water. This will help to prevent the shrimp from overcooking due to residual heat.

Peel the shrimp and discard the shells (or freeze and save them to make a seafood stock later). Arrange on a platter, serving them with your favorite cocktail sauce, a homemade traditional cocktail sauce (just grate some fresh horseradish into ketchup, then season with Worcestershire sauce, Tabasco, and lemon juice), or PK's famous Herm's Cocktail Sauce.

Herm's Cocktail Sauce

by PK

Although my grandfather Herm was friends with the best chefs in America, and was himself a food aficionado, when it came to entertaining, he relied on others to do the cooking. He preferred to watch over shoulders offering commentary along the way—an equivalent to a "backseat driver." There was however one exception—his cocktail sauce. When it came to a dipping sauce for the shrimp cocktail, he exclusively trusted the role of saucier to himself. I only knew my grandfather when I was young, so I can only vaguely remember tasting it, but the spectacle around the pink delicacy was so great that I had to try my hand at recreating it. One might describe it as a Marie Rose sauce, but in doing so you would tarnish its unique and unabashed composition. I can't promise that what I am offering lives up to Herm's, but I can promise its dominance amongst its rivals.

As I am unfamiliar with the original makeup, I won't include specific proportions. I encourage you to do what feels right. As Chris suggests, taste as you go. It should certainly have more mayo than hot sauce, more brandy than horseradish, but adjust it to your own taste, and maybe your version of Herm's sauce will be passed on through the generations as well.

Ingredients and directions:

In a bowl, add a squirt or two of ketchup, about half as much Worcestershire, and a good heaping of freshly shaved horseradish. Add the hot sauce of your choice in whatever amount is tolerable for your guests (or just go all out). Add a little mustard. We typically use a combination of Dijon and Hot English, but any mustard should get the job done (except yellow). Squeeze in lemon juice—be generous. Add mayonnaise at least equal in quantity to the rest of your ingredients.

Add salt and pepper, taste and adjust. What is it missing? Should you add more mustard? Mayo? Mix and you'll be looking at a helluva Marie Rose sauce. But we are not done.

Mix in a shot of brandy (Armagnac is best, cognac is very good too, and calvados adds a fun layer of apple). Adjust your spices once more, and you have your own version of Herm's cocktail sauce.

We are
thankful for...

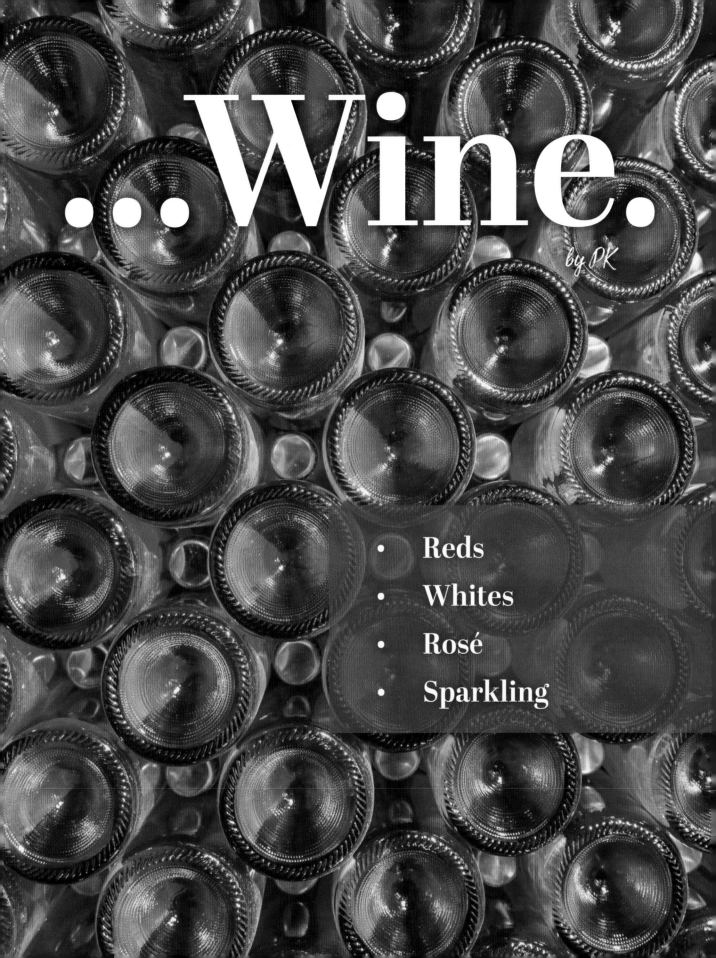

...Wine.

by PK

- Reds
- Whites
- Rosé
- Sparkling

Pairing the perfect wines
for the feast

Turkey is relatively mild in flavor, so it is important that the wine does not overwhelm it. But of course, we are not just eating turkey, we have all the delightful sides to consider. The good news is that there is an abundance of red, white, and sparkling wines that work beautifully at the Thanksgiving table.

Our goal is to pair the wines with all the flavors in the dishes.

This happens two ways. The first is by complimenting the flavors. A wine with subtle earthy notes will bring out similar flavors in the gravy, the stuffing, and the mashed potatoes (particularly if there is truffle butter involved). The second is by contrasting the flavors. Ideally, you want wines that will cut through the heaviness of many of the dishes. This is why, for red wines, ideal picks include red fruit flavors. These flavors compliment the cranberry and the greens, and together they contrast the bold, rich flavors of the heavier side dishes. For whites, clean, crisp wines with high acid accomplish the same goal. They highlight the lighter, fruiter nature of the cranberry and greens while provided a cleansing element to cut through the heavier foods.

Reds to consider

Zinfandel

Zinfandel, a popular American varietal, is right at home at the Thanksgiving table. It has the red fruit we previously discussed, while not being overwhelmingly heavy or tannic. When looking for a zin, it is important to select one that is not overripe and to avoid zins with residual sugar. As with many wines, zinfandel has undergone a transformation to appeal to a broader array of Americans. While this may benefit the sale of the wines, the consequential syrupy nature of these zins does not pair well with the Thanksgiving meal, and should be avoided.

Pinot Noir

Pinot noir's lighter body, relatively low tannins, and moderate acidity make it a great selection for Thanksgiving dinner. While California pinot noirs bring out a good deal of red fruit, those from Oregon, Washington, and most notably, Burgundy, will play more heavily on the earthy aspects of the meal.

California Pinots

These fruiter pinot noirs will typically have more upfront, bright, red fruit flavors that complement the cranberry and the sweetness of the sweet potatoes, while at the same time contrast the richer, fattier flavors of the turkey, stuffing, and gravy. Additionally, these wines are often more palatable for guests who are not typically red wine drinkers, as well as for those with palates that tend to prefer sweeter wines.

Oregon and Washington Pinots

These earthy, more mineral-rich pinot noirs stand up spectacularly to gravy, stuffing, turkey, mashed potatoes, and truffles (if you are so fortunate). While they lean toward earthy, there will inevitably be some red or dark fruit that will give the wine a beautiful edge when pairing with the cranberry sauce.

If you are looking for a budget-friendly wine, but still desire an earthier, structured pinot noir, look no further than Oregon and Washington. More so than their California cousins to the south, they closely resemble pricier Burgundies by exuding minerality and depth. Look for wines from Willamette Valley, Walla Walla, and the Columbia River Gorge in Oregon, along with Puget Sound AVA and Columbia River Gorge in Washington.

Burgundy

In my opinion, Burgundy is the brass ring of the Thanksgiving wine candidates. The only deterrent is price. Burgundy is one of the most expensive wines in the world, with some bottles reaching $20,000 (and those aren't even the collector's bottles!). If you have that kind of money, more power to you, but we typically try to stay south of 10 grand (or $30.00).

Burgundy... oh, sweet Burgundy.

Whites to consider

Sancerre, rather than sauvignon blanc

Sancerre goes particularly well with the Thanksgiving meal. Sancerre is a region in France that uses sauvignon blanc grapes to produce their wines. While these wines are made from the same varietal as New Zealand and American sauvignon blanc wines, these New World counterparts tend to place a greater emphasis on citrus notes, which can conflict with gravy in particular. Sancerre, on the other hand, has a good bit more balance and can work to cleanse the palate between bites. It leans more toward herbal than its counterparts, as well, which plays with many of the ingredients in the stuffing and the vegetable dishes.

Chenin blanc

Chenin blanc is another great white wine for the Thanksgiving table. This varietal covers an extremely wide range of finished products. When aged for long periods in oak, the result is very similar to an oak-aged chardonnay. Loire chenin is almost never aged in new oak, while oaked chenin often comes form South Africa. Baked apple and peach play with graham cracker and butterscotch, resulting in a rich, luscious wine. When the juice sees little to no time in oak, brighter, fresher notes prevail such as honeydew, hay, and jasmine. While there are sparkling and sweet styles of chenin blanc, we'll focus on the two dry and still iterations of the grape.

Oak-aged chenin blanc is great for those who typically drink chardonnay. As we've said, many of the same flavors will be present. Chenin blanc, though, is more acidic, giving it the ability to cut through the fatty aspects of the turkey while matching the acidity of the cranberry. A typical buttery chardonnay will be easily lost with the roux, and you'll find yourself struggling to distinguish between the flavors on the plate and the flavors in your glass. Oak-aged chenin blanc is the chardonnay drinker's answer to a Thanksgiving white.

On the other hand, you have chenin blanc that has spent less time in oak. This can be great if you're the kind of person who goes a little lighter on the gravy. The aforementioned hay adds a distinct element to the turkey, and jasmine adds a little something extra to the potatoes. As with the oaked chenin blanc, perhaps to an even greater extent, the acidity will play the same role of being the cranberry's equal in the realm of acidity, and cutting through the more sinful parts of the plate.

Rosé...
we could drink it all day!

Rosé is one of the most fun, popular wines in the Western world, and it has seen a massive explosion of popularity in the past two decades. It is most often thought of as a summer wine. Almost everyone loves it, but does it work on Thanksgiving? The answer is absolutely. The real question is which rosé works best on Thanksgiving. Generally, you'll want to avoid lighter or sweeter rosés, and if you want this wine to really shine, there are a few things you'll want to consider.

Rosés that are predominately made from pinot noir will play excellently next to the most famous bird of the year. These tend to be a little heavier and fuller, making sure they won't get overwhelmed by the food. They also lean on the richer side with prevalent red fruits like strawberry.

The top rosé pick must be a Bandol. Hailing from southern France, just off the Mediterranean, Bandol rosés are top of the line. Bandol is known for its red wines and rosés, and both options contain the unique blend of mourvèdre, grenache, and cinsault grapes. Mourvèdre, the third component of the very common GSM blends—grenache, syrah, and mourvèdre—so familiar to Rhône drinkers, is the least known varietal of the three, but has the richest history. Known as monestrell in Spain, historians largely agree that the wine was brought over by the Phoenicians in approximately 500 B.C. This seafaring history makes it all the more appealing for a Thanksgiving wine.

Mourvèdre is a heavier grape, and Bandol is certainly a heavier rosé. While being very deep and complex, Bandol rosé maintains a high level of acidity. This allows the wine to act two different parts in its very own one-wine play. It stands up to the hefty Thanksgiving plate like a red wine would, but its acidity and cool serving temperature add some levity to the occasion.

Don't forget the *bubbly!*

Sparkling wines are synonymous with celebration.

CHAMPAGNE

This alone is reason enough to pop open a bottle of bubbly on Thanksgiving Day.

Many love to have it as an aperitif before moving on to one of the more classically food-friendly wines for the main event. Those who do may be missing out on one of the best food pairings around.

As much as we love Thanksgiving dinner, we need to recognize it for what it is. On any other day, it would be unlikely for anyone to find this meal on the menu of a top restaurant. There are seemingly endless side dishes, all with different weights and textures, struggling for command of the plate. The sweetness of marshmallow-covered sweet potatoes seems about as far off from sausage-laden stuffing as any two restaurant courses could be, yet on Thanksgiving they occupy the same plate! After a spoonful of gravy, mashed potatoes, and crispy turkey skin, how is one to appreciate the subtleties of orange notes in the cranberry sauce?

This is where the *sparkling* wines come into play.

Many high-end restaurants will offer a palate cleanser in between courses. If the chef is moving from a rich scallop dish to a lighter chicken dish, they may include a sorbet between courses to refresh the palette, so one can take full advantage of the next dish's intricacies. Sparkling wine can play this role, as well, and not just between courses, but between bites! The effervescence of sparkling wines acts as a natural palate cleanser, tantalizing your taste buds and preparing your mouth for a completely new bite of food. On Thankgiving, this means you can move from sweet potatoes to brussels sprouts without missing a beat.

Champagne

Champagne is the world's premier sparkling wine and was already a pop culture staple when Ben Franklin was still flying kites. This timeless wine hails from central France, and can be found on restaurant menus from Beijing to Buenos Aires. Champagne's notoriety is well founded. The region boasts a wide variety of different styles, all with various tastes and applications. Blanc de Noirs Champagnes are made from exclusively red grapes, offering a fuller body. Make no mistake, though, these are still white wines! Blanc de blanc Champagnes are, for you French speakers not surprisingly, made from exclusively white grapes, resulting in a more delicate, crisp product. Then there are levels of sweetness. Brut nature is the driest, and Champagne doux is the sweetest, though there are five other levels of varying sweetness in between. Don't be fooled by Champagne that is designated as "dry"—these are actually among the sweetest, having 17-32 grams of sugar added to the bottle before corking. Finally, there is champagne rosé. To make champagne rosé, the wine is briefly exposed to the red grape skins, giving it a pinkish hue.

For Thanksgiving, Blanc de Noirs, Blanc de Blancs, and rosé Champagnes can all pair nicely.

You will most likely want to stick to the drier end of the spectrum, but this should be a relatively easy feat, as the majority of Champagne is bottled with a "brut" designation, meaning there are between 6 and 12 grams of sugar added to the bottle, leaving it well into the dry end of Champagnes. They typically pair the best with food, as they are dry enough to not overwhelm, but sweet enough to round out the flavors of the food.

A great Champagne at a reasonable price can be difficult to find. You want one that is both affordable, of great quality, and will pair well with your feast. Our favorite, checking all of the boxes, is La Caravelle Champagne Rosé. With a price point of approximately $40, it is a high quality, yet affordable option. You will find that it's more passionate than subtle, very full, and extremely memorable, with pheromonal red fruit and brioche notes coming right to the front of the palate.

This will stand up to your Thanksgiving meal without a problem.

Cava & Prosecco

As with Burgundy, the major barrier to Champagne is its price tag. It is difficult to find a bottle under $40. An easy solution to this problem is to look to other Old World sparkling wines, most notably cava, from Spain, and prosecco, from Italy.

Cava

Of the two southern European champagne alternatives, cava, a Spanish sparkling white, is more similar to Champagne from the perspective of its vinification. Cava, like Champagne, involves using up to three grape varietals. For Champagne, these include pinot noir, chardonnay, and pinot meuniere. Cava traditionally utilizes macabeo, parellada, and xarel-lo though many cavas have started to experiment with chardonnay, pinot noir, monastrell, and grenache, as well. Both wines go through their fermentation process in the bottle rather than in tanks, though Champagne typically ages longer.

The major difference between the two wines lies in the final product. Champagne typically yields a more acidic wine, while cava wines tend to lean toward the fruitier side. This has many advantages. As we discussed above, Champagne is very adaptable for food pairings, but cava's fruitier nature and lower acidity make it an excellent pairing for the Thanksgiving menu, particularly when it's contrasting the starch in the stuffing and mashed potatoes. Also, cava wines tend to have a somewhat fuller flavor than their French counterparts, adding some weight to match the heft of even the most mountainous Thanksgiving plates.

Prosecco

Prosecco hails from *Veneto,*

a region in northeastern Italy. While markedly different from Champagne and cava, prosecco wines can also make a valuable contribution to the Thanksgiving table. Utilizing a single grape varietal—glera—these wines have surpassed Champagne in worldwide sales, becoming the world's go-to sparkling wine.

Unlike Champagne and cava, prosecco undergoes its second fermentation in tanks rather than in bottles. This less expensive process yields a more delicate, lighter final product. Proseccos tend to be somewhat sweeter than cavas and Champagnes—excluding, of course, those Champagnes with particularly high amounts of added sugar—and lean toward lighter flavors such as apple, lemon, and sparkling fruit.

Prosecco is ideal for anyone who wants a strong contrast to the more indulgent aspects of the Thanksgiving meal, while introducing a particularly clean, occasionally sweet, component to the battle royal of overbearing flavors that is our favorite November meal.

Lambrusco Sparkling Red

Lambrusco has the most notoriety of the wines we've discussed thus far. Those who are familiar with the wine typically imagine sweet, almost undrinkable wines with a little bit of seemingly unnatural fizz, that can substitute for a Mad Dog 20/20. It is important to remember, however, that Chianti, Beaujolais, and even the great Burgundy each had this same low reputation in the U.S. for a time. If you know where to look, you can find a lambrusco you can be proud to serve at the Thanksgiving table, that will both captivate your guests with its somewhat exotic nature, and pair with the food in a unique and effective way. While there are white lambruscos and sweet lambruscos, for our Thanksgiving purposes we will focus on the dry, red wines lambrusco has to offer.

While some lambruscos are marked with the word secco—a surefire sign the wine was designed to be dry—some lambruscos lack either a *dulce* (sweet) or a secco designation. So it's a good practice to ask a knowledgeable employee at a wine store before buying. More often than not, we've found, they'll be excited to showcase an oft-overlooked wine, and will be happy to guide you to the right choice.

Wine glassware

As mentioned in the cocktails section, an all-purpose wine glass is good to have on hand as it can be used for both white and red wines, and even cocktails. When enjoying a particularly nice bottle on a special occasion, you may want to consider using wine glasses that have been specifically designed to enhance certain varietals.

Burgundy glass:

The burgundy glass is used for more delicate red wines, such as the eponymous wine AOC in central France. They are relatively short with a rounded bottom which curves up at the top, allowing for the more nuanced flavors to reach the nose and the mouth.

Bordeaux glass:

Used for red wines with more body, these glasses are less rounded than a burgundy glass but are taller. This glass pushes the flavor to the back of your mouth, allowing for you to experience the full force of a powerful red wine.

We are
thankful for...

...an Abundant
& Delicious
Thanksgiving Feast

by Christopher

The philosophy behind the recipes in this book

I t's important to me that the food I cook be uniquely my own. I've never been a fan of following robotic recipes that leave little room for creativity, adjustment, or personality. That's not to say that every time I turn on the stove, I create something completely original, but rather that the decisions I'm making once I turn on the stove are my own. Critics of this philosophy claim that this approach may be inaccessible for some—that only experienced cooks can find success with freestyle cooking. I wholeheartedly disagree. I believe the best way to learn is by first understanding, and then by doing. By embracing creativity and making your food your own, not only will cooking be more fun, exciting, and rewarding, but it will accelerate the speed at which you learn, and help you tackle the greatest barrier that exists between amateur cooks and realizing their potential in the kitchen—confidence.

Confidence comes from understanding the rationale behind the different cooking techniques.

For this reason, you will notice that I sometimes provide detail as to why I am using a particular technique or ingredient, rather than just telling you how to do something or how much of something to use. My intention is to provide you with a deeper understanding of each dish, which will free you up in the kitchen so you can adjust the dish to make it your own. To facilitate this, every recipe highlights opportunities for customization, allowing you to honor the Thanksgiving traditions you might have. For example, you may always use a specific spice on the turkey or a particular vegetable in the stuffing. Similarly, you may also choose to apply the techniques to improve an existing favorite recipe that has been in your family for years. Whatever your approach, be sure to take notes in the back of the book so you can replicate your brilliance next year.

It is important to note that my goal is not only to help you prepare an outstanding and memorable Thanksgiving feast, but also to provide you with some cooking insights that you can use every day. For example,

I reference the "Maillard reaction" in the context of roasting turkey, but the same concept can be applied to searing a steak or sautéing mushrooms.

You will find that the recipes are not organized in the traditional, step-by-step, chronological order. Rather, each dish is divided into sections that are key components to successfully execute the Thanksgiving meal. The idea behind this structure is to help you to internalize the approach to each dish. While some of the recipes are quick and simple, like cranberry sauce or roasted brussels sprouts, others are more substantive, like stuffing and gravy.

For the more substantive sections, I recommend that you:

- **Read (or skim)** over the chapter once to understand the rationale and approach.
- **Think** more generally about the decisions you want to make to customize the dish.
- **Take notes** of your plan, referencing the recipe to emphasize any core details or techniques you wish to apply.
- **Cook** and have fun!

Did you know?

Only male turkeys, appropriately called gobblers, actually gobble. Female turkeys cackle.

Three keys to success in the kitchen

There are a few universal concepts that will help you cook great food with less stress, regardless of what you are cooking.

Mise en place

Mise en place is a French term that translates to "set in place." In the kitchen, it refers to having all your preparation done before you begin cooking. It is the trick TV chefs use to make cooking seem so fun and effortless, and the trick restaurants use to churn out elaborate dishes in a matter of minutes. The key to success with *mis en place* is having a clear plan for what you are going to cook, and knowing exactly what you need to execute that plan. Gather everything you'll need from the fridge or cupboard, chop all your vegetables, and bring out all of the pots, pans, spatulas, and spoons you're going to need. The perfect *mis en place* will enable you to cook without ever having to leave your workstation—i.e., standing in front of your stove—because everything is within arm's reach. Mastering the art of *mis en place* will help to make cooking more enjoyable and less stressful, especially when you are cooking a feast as large as Thanksgiving.

Taste

Taste, taste, taste, then taste again! What is the easiest way to ensure the food you serve tastes good before you serve it? Taste it! This may seem obvious, but it remains an underutilized technique by many home cooks. Don't just taste your food when it is done, but taste it regularly throughout the process of cooking. This will immediately have a positive impact on your results and is a skill that can be developed and improved as you become more experienced in the kitchen. As you progress, you'll have a better understanding of exactly what adjustments can be made to perfect your food, while also gaining the ability to know what incomplete food—such as a stock that hasn't been seasoned yet—should taste like even before it's finished. One important note: do not taste raw or undercooked meat, fish, or poultry that may contain harmful bacteria. Instead, consider tasting your seasoning blend or other elements you're going to cook with it to get a sense of how the finished product will taste. Having several clean spoons on hand will also ensure that you are employing important hygiene standards.

Clean as you go

Maintain a clean and organized workstation throughout the process of preparing and cooking. If your kitchen becomes a disaster zone, cooking will become stressful and your food will suffer because you won't be able to give it the full attention it deserves. To make cleanup easier, use a large mixing bowl designated for garbage, and keep it within arm's reach. This will prevent you from having to walk across the kitchen to throw things away, or worse, leave trash around that clutters your workspace. I also like to work with two kitchen towels on hand. The first I keep tucked into a belt loop or apron strap, or throw over my shoulder, and use it to keep my hands dry and clean or to quickly grab something hot. The second towel I keep next to my cutting board, which I use to regularly wipe the board clean, wipe off anything that is stuck to my knife, and clean up small spills or messes.

And last but not least, maintain your cleanliness and organization by practicing the art of mis en place.

Let's talk turkey

Detractors of the large fowl will conjure images of dry, overcooked white meat, tough, sinewy dark meat, and soggy, soft skin. They will claim that it's impossible to achieve crispy skin while keeping the white meat moist and thoroughly cooking the tough legs. In their eyes, the turkey serves only as a vehicle for gravy, an illogical salute to tradition, or a checkmark next to the protein box. They'll claim its only redeeming aspect is its low price tag. Those detractors are so wrong.

There are a number of measures one can take to achieve
the elusive accomplishment of serving a perfect holiday bird.
For our purposes, we'll divide them into three main sections:

- Sourcing your turkey

- Preparing your turkey

- Cooking your turkey

Sourcing your turkey

The first task on your journey to turkey nirvana is buying the right bird. While the frozen supermarket fowls are both cheap and convenient, I highly recommend that you invest in the centerpiece of your meal. Recall the tale of the three little pigs and the big bad wolf? The third piglet didn't find safety in his shelter from the huffing and puffing because of superior architectural prowess, but rather because he made an investment in high-quality material—bricks. The Thanksgiving equivalent to building your house out of sturdy bricks is to buy a fresh, heritage breed turkey. Check out chapter IV for more thoughts on this.

Preparing your turkey

Once you have your perfect bird, it's time to roll up your sleeves and get down to business. For our purposes, we'll focus on roasting the turkey. While frying, smoking, or other advanced techniques that involve confits, braises, or roulades may yield a delicious meal, roasting brings to the table a traditional holiday Thanksgiving-y-ness that can't be beat, while remaining accessible to experts and beginners alike, and with no need for advanced equipment or skill.

We are all too familiar with the typical shortcomings of poorly roasted turkeys—the white meat is dry, the dark meat is tough, and the skin is soggy. By keeping these common failings in mind, we can devise a plan that will prevent our beautiful bird from falling into Thanksgiving mediocrity.

Cooking your turkey

Our preferred method: butchering your turkey

First let's address the fact that the turkey is not uniform in its makeup. The turkey's legs are made up of dark meat, which is more flavorful, but also has more collagen and sinew, making the drumsticks tough if they are not thoroughly cooked. On the other hand, the turkey's breasts, made up of white meat, are much leaner and more tender, putting them at risk of drying out if overcooked. As Occom's razor would suggest, the simplest solution here is the best solution—cook them separately. We cannot in good conscience take two quite different types of meat and suggest that one cooking method is sufficient. By butchering the turkey into its parts, you can give the legs the low and slow treatment they deserve, and perfectly roast the breasts at a much higher temperature for a much shorter time. In addition, when the turkey is broken down into its parts, you can roast all of it skin-side-up, as opposed to roasting a whole turkey with the breasts facing up and the thighs facing mostly down. This will help to ensure that all skin is perfectly and evenly browned. Separating the carcass from the meat also allows you to use the carcass and trimmings in your stock (see below). Furthermore, this technique can be beneficial for particularly large turkeys or particularly small ovens, as the smaller individual pieces will allow you to play a game of turkey Tetris to find their best fit.

In summary, there are four good reasons to butcher your turkey in advance of cooking:

- The legs and wings can be cooked low and slow for tender dark meat

- The white meat can be cooked at a high temperature for a shorter period of time for juicy white meat

- Everything can be roasted skin side up for crispier skin

- Smaller ovens can more easily accommodate larger turkeys

Did you know?

Butterball receives almost 100,000 calls on their Turkey Talk Line each year. If you follow Chris' techniques outlined in this chapter we know you won't be one of them.

How to Butcher Your Turkey

If you have never butchered a chicken or a turkey, it might seem like a daunting task. No worries, I've got your back. Read the instructions, look at the pictures, and if you are a visual learner, visit our website to watch a video.

First, start with a clean and clear countertop. Put your cutting board on top of a wet cloth or paper towel to help secure it. I recommend plastic cutting boards over wooden ones for raw meat—they are easier to sterilize. Have a tray ready for the turkey pieces, as well as a bowl or tray for the scraps and carcass which you'll want to save for your stock. You'll need a sturdy, sharp chef's knife, a paring knife, and a cloth or paper towel.

When you're ready

Dry the turkey. Pat the outside of the turkey dry with your cloth or paper towel.

Remove the innards

Assuming they came with the bird. Typically, they are found in a plastic or mesh bag inside the turkey's carcass. Put the neck in your scraps bowl for stock. The kidneys and heart can also be added to the stock or to the gravy, or pan-fried for a delicious snack to reward yourself for butchering a turkey! The liver should not be added to the stock, as it will become bitter if it's boiled. Fry it up with the kidneys and livers, or save it to make pâté.

Remove the wishbone

Use your hand to feel the bone in the front of the breasts—the head end, not the tail end. It is shaped like an upside down "V." Use your paring knife to make a cut on either side of the bone, then slide your thumb and index finger into the slits, slide them up the bone to separate it from the meat and pull the bone out. Be careful, as it breaks easily and can be sharp if broken. Place it in your bowl of scraps or set it aside to dry it out and wish on it later.

Remove the legs

Using your chef's knife, make a slit in the skin between the drumstick and the breast. I like to make the slit as close as possible to the leg, making sure to leave plenty of skin to cover the top of the breast. Now grab the leg and pull it away from the turkey, bending it outward until the thighbone pops out of the joint on the backbone.

Use your chef's knife to cut along the backbone and through the joint to separate the leg from the turkey. When you make this cut, be sure to cut around the oyster, keeping it attached to the thigh rather than the carcass. The oyster is one of the tastiest bits on the turkey. In France it is called *sot-l'y-laisse*, which means "the fool leaves it there." You wouldn't want the French to think you're a fool, would you? Repeat on the other side.

French the legs

This is optional—frenching is purely for aesthetic purposes. With a turkey, the meat will likely pull off the bone anyway, but frenching will give you a cleaner bone and a more refined look. Using your chef's knife, cut around the bone about one inch from the foot end of the drumstick. Use a paper towel to grip the cartilage and skin at the end of the drumstick and pull it off. Use your paring knife or a pair of kitchen shears to sever any stubborn tendons and to clean up the bone. Cover any exposed bone with tinfoil to prevent it from scorching when it is roasted.

Remove the wings

Grab the wing and pull it away from the breast to locate the joint between the wing and the breast. Use your chef's knife to cut cleanly through this joint. Repeat on the other side. If you'd like, remove the wing tips by cutting cleanly through the joint between them and the flat of the wing. Put the wing tips in your scraps bowl for stock and put the wings aside on your tray.

Remove the breasts

Lift the tip of the breasts (so that the tail end faces up), and cut down through the rib cage separating the majority of the ribcage from the breast and breastplate. This portion—the two breasts attached to the breast plate—is called the crown. Set the whole crown on your tray and reserve the carcass to use for stock.

Trim excess skin

Checking each piece of the turkey, find any uneven, excessive flaps of skin, and trim them away conservatively by slicing through the skin with your chef's knife. Don't be overly aggressive with the trimming—the skin will shrink and pull back as the turkey cooks, so a little excess is fine.

Remove the turkey tail from the carcass

This is also optional. Use your chef's knife to cut cleanly through the spine where it meets the tail. Affectionately referred to as the "turkey's ass" in my family, the tail is an oft-forgotten, delectably fatty morsel. I like to think of it as the turkey's best impersonation of pork belly. If you do save it from the anticlimactic fate of boiling away in your stock, prepare and cook it along with the dark meat, and savor it with a lucky friend or relative in the kitchen before serving the turkey to the rest of the gang.

Addressing other techniques

Traditionally, a Thanksgiving turkey is roasted whole. Advocates for this technique will often reference tradition and presentation because, typically, they enjoy carving the bird at the table. On presentation, I believe a well-carved and properly garnished platter of turkey can go toe-to-toe with any whole turkey, and should have no problem garnering a chorus of "Ooohs" and "Aaahs" from your awe-inspired guests. If tableside carving is an unalienable institution and foundational to the traditions of your family's feast, then I recommend leaving the two breasts whole together. The carving of the large, heart-shaped centerpiece known as the turkey's crown should be of sufficient spectacle to please even the staunchest traditionalist.

Not convinced?
Here are some recommendations for cooking a turkey whole... if you must.

- Make sure to season the inside of the carcass in addition to the outside of turkey. You may also wish to fill the hollow cavity with aromatics such as a head of garlic, quartered onions, halved lemons, or bunches of herbs like sage, rosemary, and thyme. I do not recommend filling the inside of your turkey with your stuffing, which is much better prepared in a casserole.

- Truss the turkey with butcher's twine to seal the cavity and hold the legs up. This helps hot air pass under the legs in the oven, which allows the legs to cook more easily and the skin to brown.

- Either remove the wing tips or tuck them underneath the breasts. Do not let them sit on top of the breasts or they will burn, while also preventing the breasts from properly browning.

- Regularly rotate the turkey within the oven by flipping it upside down. This will help the turkey brown more evenly, and work to prevent the breasts from drying out too much. Just make sure to finish breast-side-up so the skin on the breasts doesn't get overly soggy.

Spatchcock you say?

Recently, the technique of spatchcocking one's Thanksgiving turkey has garnered a large, enthusiastic following. Spatchcocking—a more fun way of saying butterflying—involves cutting out the turkey's backbone, pulling it open, and pressing down on the breasts to crack the breastplate so it lays flat. Proponents argue that doing this allows the meat to cook more evenly and exposes more of the skin, resulting in more even browning. I would counter that those same advantages are achieved at an even higher level with my preferred method of breaking down the bird completely. I consider spatchcocking to be a half-measure compared to the superior technique of fully butchering the turkey. Spatchcocking fails to allow for separate cooking of the white and dark meat, often leads to awkward carving due to parts of the ribcage being attached to the thighs, and leaves less of the carcass to use for stock. Most important, roasting trays and ovens large enough to hold a sizeable spatchcocked turkey are few and far between. In our kitchen we have a professional Garland stove from the 1950s—yes, the same model as Julia's—and back in my spatchcocking days we had a hard time fitting our large bird even in that enormous oven.

Brining your turkey

Brining a turkey is a critical technique to help it retain moisture as it cooks. Typically, there are two types of brine—dry, and wet. Dry brining involves sprinkling your turkey with salt and other dry spices, powders, or seasonings. Wet brining involves submerging your turkey into a solution of salt and sugar dissolved in water, often with spices, herbs, aromatics, or seasonings. My experience is that dry brining is the superior technique, resulting in both better texture and more concentrated flavor.

In order to dry brine your turkey, you'll first want to create a rub. Start off with kosher salt and baking powder. These will help dry out the skin of your turkey, which will allow for the Maillard reaction to begin more quickly, since less time is wasted in the oven evaporating water from the skin. The salt will also season the meat as it is absorbed. Meanwhile, the baking powder has the added benefit of raising the pH level of the surface of the skin, making it more alkaline, which reduces the temperature of the Maillard reaction, allowing browning to begin more quickly. Feel free to add spices, powders, and dried herbs to your rub, using a fork or small whisk to thoroughly combine the ingredients.

Maillard Reaction

The Maillard reaction is the result of sugars and proteins having a chemical reaction at high temperatures.

It is what gives cooked foods a brown color and distinct umami-laden flavor. For those unfamiliar, umami is the fifth category of taste in food (like sweet, bitter, etc.) corresponding to the flavor of amino acids such as monosodium glutamate. Seared steaks, fried potatoes, bread crust, sauteed mushrooms, and marshmallows roasted over a campfire all benefit from the Maillard reaction. While you don't need to know the chemistry that goes on behind the scenes of your Thanksgiving dinner, it is helpful to understand a few keys to take full advantage of the Maillard reaction.

- Water prevents the reaction from occurring quickly, so starting with a dry surface can help you get a better sear on your food.

- The reaction happens more quickly with a higher pH, so alkaline foods sear at a faster rate than acid foods. Using baking powder or baking soda can raise the pH, helping to get a great crust on ingredients, while marinades with a lot of lemon or vinegar might make browning more challenging.

- While the reaction can happen over long periods of time at relatively low temperatures—such as with black garlic, which is cooked for around 90 days at 180°F—it really kicks in at temperatures greater than 280-330°F. Higher temperatures will make the reaction happen more quickly.

- Taking the reaction too far will lead to pyrolysis—aka burning. This is when food goes from brown to black and becomes very bitter. Obviously, we want to avoid pyrolysis.

My Rub Recipe

Creating your own rub is one of the best ways to personalize your turkey. You can include your favorite flavor combinations with the spices that you love and, in doing so, put your own stamp and personality into your food. Don't feel obligated to limit yourself to the traditional Thanksgiving flavors if you want to get creative and have some fun with it.

That being said, here's my rub. Don't think of this as a recipe to follow, but rather as an example from which you can build. The only constants that you should make sure to keep are the salt and baking powder. I like to keep my rub relatively simple to allow the turkey to shine.

Ingredients:

- ½ cup kosher salt
- 1 tsp baking powder
- 1 tbs onion powder
- 1 tbs garlic powder
- 1 tbs MSG (monosodium glutamate)

I find the onion and garlic powders give a nice traditional, Thanksgiving-y flavor that works really well to provide an extra dimension to the skin, while the MSG acts as a burst of umami flavor that will keep your guests coming back for seconds. You'll notice I left out black pepper—I personally prefer black pepper to be freshly cracked, so I wait to use my pepper mill on Thanksgiving morning before placing the turkey in the oven. The amount of rub you use will depends on the size of your turkey, and this recipe will probably yield much more than you need. I always err on the side of making too much rub and saving what is left in an airtight container like a spice jar, to use on future poultry roasts.

Once your rub is ready, generously season each piece of your turkey, taking care to season the bottoms and sides as well. Cover two large sheet pans with a few layers of heavy-duty tinfoil and set wire racks in the sheets. Place the turkey parts onto the wire racks with the breasts on one tray, and the legs, wings, and tail on another. The tinfoil will help to prevent too much heat from radiating up from the sheet pan into the bottom of the meat and will also make cleanup easier. Seasoning the meat before setting it on the tray will prevent too much salt from collecting on the tray, which would make the pan drippings far too salty to use in your gravy. Set the trays in your refrigerator, uncovered. By sitting uncovered, the skin on your turkey will begin to dry out, which, as mentioned before, will allow for the Maillard reaction to get started immediately when cooking. Conveniently, these are the trays that you will use to roast the turkey, so your preparation on Thanksgiving morning will be minimal, allowing you to focus on the other components of the meal.

Cooking the bird to perfection

You scored the perfect bird, delicately butchered it with exacting precision, and masterfully seasoned it. You're teed up for a home run, and all that's left is to swing the bat. While all of the work you've put in so far sets you up for success, there are a few things you're going to want to keep in mind to make sure you execute the cooking to perfection.

Tempering your turkey

Before putting the turkey in the oven, there are a couple more steps to keep in mind that will guarantee your fowl's successful roast. Since the dark meat is cooked first, it gets the treatment first.

One hour before going into the oven, take the meat out of the refrigerator to temper. Letting the meat come to room temperature before roasting will provide a couple of benefits that work toward our goal of not drying out the bird. Doing so helps the meat cook more evenly by reducing the amount of work the oven has to do to get the interior of the meat up to temperature, and therefore it reduces the discrepancy in time between when the exterior and interior of the meat are cooked through. If there is too large a discrepancy, the meat closer to the surface will start to overcook while the meat's center will still be raw or underdone. When the turkey is plunged into a high temperature environment like an oven, it's shocked by the drastic change, and the muscle fibers tense up. By bringing the turkey up to room temperature before putting it into the oven, you can reduce the intensity of this shock and prevent the meat from loosing precious juices.

Adding fat

Before putting the turkey into the oven, you'll want to protect it by rubbing it down with a type of fat. This will help to prevent the meat from drying out, while dispersing heat to help the skin brown evenly. There are three types of fat from which to choose for this step.

Clarified butter

Who doesn't love butter? Butter is an emulsion of butterfat, dairy solids, and water. Because of its makeup, however, two problems arise—the water, and the dairy solids. The water is an issue because you just air-dried the turkey's skin in your refrigerator so it can begin browning in the oven immediately. It makes no sense at this point to rub the skin with something that contains water.

The dairy solids are an issue because they'll burn before the turkey is cooked through. This will give off a bitter flavor and create an unappealing presentation.

Of course, butter lovers would never let such trivial issues get in the way of their favorite fat. They would find a solution! By clarifying the butter, you can isolate the butterfat and remove the water and dairy solids. Alternatively, you can use clarified, browned butter known as ghee.

Oil

Using oil to cover your turkey is great because it is easy. It doesn't need to be softened, melted, or clarified. In fact, it's probably already sitting in your pantry, so you'll have one less item on your grocery list. While any cooking oil works, pick one with a smoke point higher than the highest temperature your oven will be set at to cook your turkey (see below). This will help the skin brown evenly while avoiding unwanted bitter flavors from the oil burning. Skip over the high-priced finishing oils like first-press extra-virgin olive oils. Their flavors will fade in the oven and you won't see as significant a return on your investment as you would by drizzling it over a finished dish.

Animal Fat

Anyone who has fried their eggs in leftover bacon grease when making Sunday breakfast knows that Emeril Lagasse isn't lying when he proclaims, "Pork fat rules!" Animal fats are packed with flavor. In fact, many of the flavor enzymes that make various meats taste great come from the fat—one of the many reasons well-marbled steaks taste so good. Because these fats are so potent, you'll want to stick with fowl fats and avoid overpowering beef or pork fat (sorry, Emeril). Because it is highly unlikely your butcher sells rendered turkey fat, your best bets are chicken fat—also known as schmaltz—and my personal favorite...drum roll please... duck fat. I like to get a tub of D'Artanian duck fat, which is readily available in most high-end supermarkets.

Rub your fat of choice all over each piece of meat to make sure the entire surface area is well coated. If you are using any herbs or spices, such as freshly cracked black pepper, that you have left out out of your dry brine, go ahead and season the turkey with them now.

Smoke point

The smoke point of a fat is the temperature at which it releases smoke. Taking a fat to its smoke point can lead to unwanted, bitter flavors. Taking a fat beyond its smoke point can cause a fire. Thus, fats with high smoke points are necessary for high heat cooking like sautéing or frying.

Some high-quality fats, like extra-virgin olive oils, begin to lose the intricacies of their flavor at temperatures well below their smoke point, and should be reserved for drizzling onto food after its finished cooking.

Common fats and their smoke points:

Fat	Temperature (°F)
Butter	302°F
Clarified butter	482°F
Canola oil	428°F
Olive oil	320-405°F depending on the oil
Peanut oil	441°F
Grapeseed oil	421°F
Vegetable oil	428°F
Chicken fat	375°F
Duck fat	375°F
Pork fat	375°F

Arranging aromatics

Arrange your aromatics around the turkey to roast with it.

I like to use:

- Red onions, peeled and cut into wedges
- Shallots, peeled and cut into wedges
- Whole garlic heads, with the tops trimmed off
- Lemons, cut into wedges
- Oranges, cut into wedges
- Bouquets of thyme, rosemary, and sage

Like the meat, you can protect the *aromatics* by coating them in a fat.

I recommend using an inexpensive, neutral oil for this, such as vegetable or canola oil. Your choice of fat is a lot less important for the aromatics than it is for the turkey, so stick with what's cheap and easy. The easiest way to coat them is to take a small plate or bowl, fill it with a layer of oil and roll each piece of onion, garlic, shallot, or citrus in it before arranging them on the tray. Alternatively, you can spray them with an oil sprayer. Tuck them between and all around the pieces of meat, trying to distribute them as evenly as you can. When roasting, their pungent aromas will fill up the oven, flavoring the air that cooks the turkey. After roasting, save the aromatics—they will make beautiful garnishes to arrange with your turkey, and will take your presentation to the next level.

It is also worth noting that your guests will likely be arriving while the turkey is still in the oven, so their first peek of the turkey will be on the roasting tray. Having these beautiful garnishes and aromas will help your turkey create a first impression that is sure to wow. Being able to present a polished and attractive finished product is impressive, but being able to present a polished and attractive product that is still in the works…well that's genius.

Adding moisture

Finally, pour one-quarter to one-half cup of water into the tray, depending on the size of the tray. You want just enough water to cover the whole bottom in a very thin layer. Try to avoid pouring any water directly onto the meat or aromatics. The water will steam up into the bottom of the turkey pieces, helping to create a moist environment in which the meat won't dry out. It will also prevent pan drippings from burning or scorching, protecting your gravy from having burned, bitter flavors. Because the water will evaporate in the hot oven, you may have to replenish it once or twice during the roasting process.

Time and temperature

Preheat the oven to 275°F. As with great barbecue, this low and slow temperature will break down all of the toughness and collagen in the legs without drying out the meat. But also as with barbecue, it will take a long time. Regularly rotate the roasting tray if your oven has hot spots or heats inconsistently. The exact time is dependent on the size of your turkey, but the sweet spot typically falls between 4-6 hours, and cooking at this low temperature provides a lot of leeway. You can feel comfortable that the dark meat is ready when the skin has browned and the meat is tender to the touch and juicy. It doesn't have to be fall-off-the bone, shredding-when-you-pull-it tender, but it should be tender enough that it is easy to eat. Don't be afraid to take the roasting tray out of the oven and touch the meat to check its doneness.

If you have an oven big enough to fit the white meat tray next to the dark meat, put the white meat in the oven when you have about an hour left on the dark meat. If not, don't worry, you can start the white meat after the dark comes out, just plan your cooking schedule accordingly. With the oven still set at 275°F, it will gently cook the breasts up to temperature. Unlike the dark meat, however, the breasts will not be in the oven for long enough to develop a crispy brown skin at this temperature. By finishing the breasts with a quick blast in the oven at 500°F, you can quickly brown the skin without raising the internal temperature too high that the meat becomes dry. This technique of using low heat to bring meat up to temperature slowly, then using high heat to quickly brown the outside, is called a reverse-sear. It is very popular with steaks, and is conceptually very similar to sous-vide, or vacuum-sealed cooking.

To execute this technique, take the white meat out of the oven once its internal temperature registers with a meat thermometer around 135°F. Don't worry, the carryover cooking from residual heat and the sear will get the temperature up to a safe 165°F. Crank the oven up to 500°F and wait at least ten minutes for it to get hot. If your oven has convection, now is the time to turn it on. Place the white meat back in the oven and let it roast for around 10 minutes, keeping an eye on it to make sure it doesn't scorch. Be warned, this step will likely produce a good amount of smoke. If you live in an apartment or smaller space and want to avoid smoke, use a slightly lower temperature, around 450°F. Rotate the tray part of the way through cooking if it is not browning evenly.

If your dark meat hasn't taken on as much color as you would like, or has gotten a little too cool while you were finishing the white meat, feel free to put it back in the oven for a couple of minutes, but be careful, it will dry out quickly if left in for more than 5-10 minutes.

Resting your turkey

It is critically important that you allow your turkey to rest for one hour before you carve it. While it's resting, the carryover heat will continue to cook the turkey, and the cooling meat will begin to relax. When the turkey comes out of the oven, the hot muscle fibers in the meat are very tense. If you were to cut into the turkey now, the tense fibers would not be able to retain very much moisture, causing turkey juices to spill out onto your cutting board rather than remain inside the meat.

Caution!

The most difficult part of roasting the perfect turkey may be in these very moments. You may find yourself alone in the kitchen, the scent of aromatics and poultry filling the room, staring down at the deep golden-brown skin. You'll ask yourself, "Will anyone really notice if I trim a little end off of the thigh?" Don't do it! Take a deep breath and a bite of stuffing if you must, but leave the turkey alone to rest.

Carving your turkey

Because we've separated the turkey into its parts before roasting, most of the work is already done. To carve the turkey, you'll need a sharp, chef's knife and a cutting board. Having rested the turkey for an hour, it should be cool enough to handle and relaxed enough so there is no significant juice runoff. I do, however like to keep a kitchen towel or paper towel by my side just in case.

Step-by-Step Guide to Carving

Please see our website for videos.

Separate the drumstick from the thigh

Cut through the joint with your chef's knife. If your knife hits the bone, don't try to force it through. Pull the knife out and try again, adjusting to find the joint. If you don't feel confident that you're going to find the joint on your first try, turn the leg over (skin side down). It's no big deal if you make a mess of the bottom of the leg, but it will adversely affect your presentation if you tear up the skin side. The drumsticks can be served whole, so once they are separated from the thighs, they are ready for presentation.

Carve the thighs

The first step to carving the thighs is to remove the bone. There is one bone that runs the length of the thigh. Turn the meat skin side down and use your knife to cut on either side of it, angling inward, so you can pull the bone out leaving as little meat on it as possible. Discard this bone or set it aside for making stock at a later date. Lay the thigh meat flat and slice it, using one long stroke of the knife for each cut, if possible. Repeat the process with the other leg.

Address the breasts

Make a cut through the skin in the direct center between the two breasts. Continuing to make gentle cuts using long, smooth strokes with your knife, cut along the side of the bone between the breasts. Work your way downward and then outward along the bone until you have separated the breast meat from any bone. Turn the breast skin-side down to observe the direction of the grain so you know how to slice perpendicular, or against, it. Return the breast to be skin side up and slice the meat using one long stroke to make each cut, if possible. The more strokes back and forth you make with your knife, the less clean the cut will be.

Try to angle your knife slightly forward and have the outward side of the breast facing toward you. The side you just cut to carve the breast off of the carcass should face away from you. This will leave the skin attached at the bottom until you have completed your cut, thus preventing the friction of your blade from separating the skin from the turkey. When deciding on the thickness of each slice, think about what you would want on your plate. Don't go too thin, because you want a meaty bite and a generous bit of skin, but don't go too thick, either, because even a modest portion of turkey can become an overwhelming feast by the time all of the side dishes are piled onto the plate.

When moving your sliced breast to the serving tray, slide your knife under the breast, using it like a long spatula, and use your other hand for support. Carefully move the breast as a whole, then slide it off the knife with your support hand. This is much easier than moving the individual slices one by one and will provide for a cleaner presentation. Repeat the process with the other breast.

Present the wings

The wings can be presented as they are, or you can separate the drumette from the flat by cutting through the joint, just as you did when separating the thigh and drumstick.

Reward yourself and close friends with the tail

The tail can be divided into however many pieces necessary for your adventurous eaters. It has small bones that shouldn't be a problem to cut through, but make sure everyone is careful of them when eating it. I personally recommend keeping the tail as an in-the-kitchen snack, a reward for all your hard work. In my family we split it between my brother, my cousins, and myself, eating it as a toast to our uncle, who first told us about this delicious but oft-neglected delicacy.

Presenting Your Turkey

As a painter must choose their canvas, your first task is to pick the right platter on which to present your turkey. The most important factor to consider is the size of the platter. You want it large enough to hold all the turkey, but not so large that it visually dwarfs the meat, removing the sense of abundance that is core to the Thanksgiving culinary aesthetic. I tend to prefer oval platters, as they highlight the natural curves of the carved turkey parts.

Before you start plating, be sure to have everything within arm's reach. You should have the platter, the carved turkey, the roasted aromatics, and some fresh herbs such as parsley, sage, rosemary, or thyme. Tie some of the herbs together with butchers' twine to create several bouquets garnis. I like to tie each one tightly around the stems and fan out the leaves for presentation.

Because they're the largest, I add the breasts to the platter first. As mentioned in the carving section, move each carved breast as a whole, rather than reconstructing it on the platter slice by slice. Don't feel you need to put the two breasts next to each other or follow some kind of white-meat-on-the-left, dark-on-the-right rule. Creating layers in which garnishes of herbs or roasted aromatics are tucked around the meat will help to provide visual intrigue. For the cleanest appearance, tuck them between different kinds of pieces, such as between a thigh and a breast, rather than between two slices of a single type. I like to lean the drumsticks together, bones facing up, to add vertical dimension to the plate.

Turkey Timeline

8-12 days before Thanksgiving:

- Buy turkey if frozen
- Start defrosting turkey

2-3 days before Thanksgiving:

- Buy turkey if fresh
- Butcher turkey
- Dry brine turkey

6 hours before dinner:

- Take the dark meat out to temper
- Preheat the oven to 275°F

5 hours before dinner:

- Dark meat goes into the oven

2 hours before dinner:

- Dark meat comes out and white meat goes into the oven

About an hour before dinner:

- If needed, sear the skin at 450-500°F for 10 minutes
- Take white meat out of oven and set turkey aside to rest

Just before dinner:

- Carve the turkey

Thanksgiving Stock

Turkey stock is the backbone of a successful Thanksgiving feast— and, coincidentally, the best way to use the backbone of your turkey. But we'll get to that. Stock is the core ingredient of Thanksgiving gravy, and is central to the stuffing and green bean casserole. The cohesive flavors of your Thanksgiving plate will emanate largely from stock, so the store-bought boxes and cans simply won't do. In fact, making your own home-made stock is arguably the single most impactful upgrade you can make to step up your Thanksgiving meal.

What is stock?

Stock is flavorful liquid made by simmering water with meat and vegetables for a long period of time.

What's the difference between stock and broth?

Stock, unlike broth, includes bones and excludes salt. The bones release gelatin into the liquid, giving it more body, and the lack of salt allows you to reduce it as much as you'd like without it becoming too salty. Broth is intended to be consumed as is (at most, you would add a few ingredients to make a simple soup). Stock is intended to be used as an ingredient, incorporated into sauces or dishes to give them flavor and texture.

What type of stock is a Thanksgiving stock?

It's a brown turkey stock. It's brown because we're encouraging darker roasted flavors which will make the stock darker in color, as opposed to a white stock, which would be lighter in both flavor and color. Reinforcing warm, darker roasted flavors is consistent with most of the dishes in our Thanksgiving feast. This will help give the meal a more cohesive feel. It's a turkey stock because turkey is the primary flavor in this meal. Incorporating a turkey-flavored stock in side dishes like the stuffing and the gravy helps them compliment the turkey itself, tying everything together around the centerpiece of the feast.

Our goal is...

to maximize the depth, complexity, and strength of our stock's flavor, while maintaining a distinctly Thanksgiving profile. Our game plan to achieve this includes three steps:

- **Getting the right ingredients**
- **Enhancing their flavor**
- **Extracting their flavor**

Complexity

What makes food complex?

Complex food has multiple flavors present in one bite. Complexity can be achieved by layering together different flavors. Layering is a chef-y term for deliberately combining ingredients with unique flavors in order to form a cohesive flavor profile. Natural complexity can also be found in individual ingredients, especially if they are umami-rich like truffles, or are created with time by fermenting or aging the ingredients, such as with kimchi or wine, or by applying heat to the ingredients and causing the Maillard reaction (see definition on page 97).

Why is that a good thing?

We like complexity because it makes food more interesting. Complex dishes require us to stop and think. They can evolve with every bite, wake up different taste buds, and can even evoke an emotional response.

So, is simple food bad?

No, simplicity can also be wonderful, and can be a brilliant way to celebrate high quality ingredients by letting them shine on their own. But for the purposes of making stock, we are combining a number of lower-quality bits of meat and vegetables to build something greater than the sum of its parts. So, in this case we want to avoid simplicity in favor of complexity.

Take Stock of Your Ingredients

Our stock will be made up of four key components:

- Protein
- Vegetables
- Herbs & Spices
- Water

Protein

The protein gives the stock its primary flavor, body, and color. Meat largely provides flavor, while bones and joints give off gelatin that provides texture. The perfect stock balances the use of both. Obviously, for Thanksgiving the turkey provides the primary protein. If you have decided to break down the bird a couple of days before Thanksgiving (as recommended on pages 93-95), you will already have a great starting point. The carcass is perfect for stock. Feel free to supplement the carcass with some additional poultry. I sometimes add chicken, which is often more readily available than turkey. If you want an extra layer of complexity, smoked turkey legs or even a ham hock can bring unique flavors to the stock. Alternatively, to be more cost-effective, freeze leftover carcasses, meat, or bones from meals involving chicken or turkey in the months leading up to Thanksgiving and use those. Personally, I use a combination of my turkey carcass, frozen leftover chicken carcasses, and fresh poultry meat from the grocery store to give my stock a strong base at a reasonable cost.

"Gratitude unlocks the fullness of life. It turns what we have into enough, and more. It turns denial into acceptance, chaos to order, confusion to clarity. It can turn a meal into a feast, a house into a home, a stranger into a friend. It turns problems into gifts, failures into successes, the unexpected into perfect timing, and mistakes into important events. It can turn an existence into a real life, and disconnected situations into important and beneficial lessons. Gratitude makes sense of our past, brings peace for today, and creates a vision for tomorrow."

~Melody Beattie

Which meats should go into stock?

Meat	Description
Turkey carcass	Excellent for stock and especially convenient if you've already butchered your turkey. The carcass will provide great flavor and texture.
Turkey neck	Excellent for stock. Necks will provide great flavor and texture. It's likely that one came with the turkey, but if you're lucky you may be able to find extras at the market.
Turkey innards	Excellent for stock…if you're into that kind of thing. Innards will add a unique flavor to the stock, which some people find too strong, but if you enjoy innards or giblet gravy, they bring a lot of flavor to the meal. Use the gizzard and heart, but do not use the liver—it will become bitter when it cooks in the stock.
Turkey legs	Excellent for stock. The leg meat may be tougher than other parts of the bird, but it's the most flavorful. You can often find turkey legs in the supermarket, and they are a great value.
Turkey breasts	Not for stock. Breasts are primarily favored for the tenderness of the meat, which does little good for a stock. They have a high price point that isn't justified by any benefits they would provide to a stock.
Turkey wings	Excellent for stock. The wings are flavorful and packed with collagen, which will give off gelatin to lend body and richness.
Turkey feet/paws	Excellent for stock. The feet are packed full of collagen, which will give off gelatin to lend body and richness.
Smoked turkey legs	An interesting way to add a unique layer of flavor to stock. Smoked legs have similar benefits to raw legs, but with an additional smokey flavor. In small doses this can add nice complexity to the stock, but too much smoked meat will overpower the stock with smokey flavor, to the point of becoming unpleasantly bitter. Use smoked turkey legs sparingly or omit them altogether if you prefer a more traditional flavor profile.
Chicken	Chicken has a similar flavor to turkey. It is also readily available in most supermarkets, and the parts most useful for a stock tend to be cheap. For these reasons, supplementing your turkey stock with some chicken can be convenient. The above descriptions of the different parts of a turkey can also be applied to the respective parts of a chicken. When considering the quantity of chicken vs. turkey, remember that, at the end of the day, you're making a turkey stock supplemented with chicken, not the other way around.
Smoked ham hock	An interesting way to add a unique layer of flavor to stock. With a different profile from the other meats on the list, ham hocks can add complexity. Similar to smoked turkey legs, smoked ham hocks should be used sparingly to avoid overpowering the stock with smoke and ham flavors, and should be omitted if you prefer a more traditional flavor profile.

Vegetables for Stock

While the protein gives the primary flavor to the stock, vegetables can add layers of flavor that enhance the complexity while also helping to lend the stock some extra color. *In the spirit of keeping the flavor profile Thanksgiving-y, the best place to start is with mirepoix.*

Mirepoix

Mirepoix is a French term for the combination of onion, carrot, and celery. Depending on whom you ask, the ratio can range from three equal parts to two parts onion, one part carrot, and one part celery. For the onion, use white, yellow, or Spanish rather than Vidalia or red onions. Cooked together, the flavors combine, and the bitterness of the celery balances out the sweetness of the onion and carrot. The vegetal mixture is foundational to countless dishes in all areas of Western cuisine. In Italian, Spanish, and Latin American cuisines, the combination is called sofrito. In Louisiana, they use a modified version and call it the Holy trinity. Holy trinity replaces the carrot with bell pepper, which is much easier to grow in Louisiana. It is a perfectly acceptable replacement for mirepoix if it's a part of your family's tradition...or if the Saints are playing. On Thanksgiving, mirepoix is often mixed into stuffing, and plays a critical role in the stock. Its flavors are quintessential to the Thanksgiving experience, permeating throughout the meal.

Beyond mirepoix, continue to add other vegetables that are consistent with the flavor profile of the meal. Think garlic, shallots, leeks, and parsnips or other root vegetables. For a rich umami-packed stock, throw in some dried mushrooms as well. Don't worry about how you dice the vegetables, just give them a rough chop to increase the surface area and ensure they fit into your stockpot. Good news! You don't have to worry about peeling the onions or garlic, as it will all be strained anyway, and the skins actually help add color to the stock. In fact, the stock is a great place to use scraps and trimmings, like mushroom stems, celery stalk butt ends, tips, and tails, and peeled skins of trimmed carrots or onions. If you want to be extra sustainable and low waste, save and freeze your vegetable trimmings from meals you cook in the month leading up to Thanksgiving and use those along with your fresh vegetables.

Herbs and spices

More subtle than the meats and vegetables, herbs and spices will help to build upon the flavor profile, elevating the stock with just the right je ne sais quoi. As with the vegetables, keep in mind that the stock will be strained, so you don't need to grind the spices or remove stems from the herbs. In fact, I encourage you to use the stems from the herbs as they typically have more flavor than the leaves. When possible, use fresh herbs, and keep in mind the traditional flavors of Thanksgiving such as parsley, thyme, sage, bay leaf, and rosemary, and spices like whole black peppercorns, coriander seeds, and fennel seeds. Avoid spices that may become overpowering, like whole cinnamon sticks.

Enhancing the flavor

Before combining the ingredients into a stock, there are steps you can take to concentrate and enhance the flavor. Given that robust flavor is the goal of a great stock, these steps are essential for taking the stock the extra mile and elevating your entire meal. Heat is the primary tool through which we execute these steps.

First, roast the stock meat.
Preheat your oven to 450°F. Use a roasting tray with high enough walls that you'll be able to fill it with water to deglaze after roasting. We'll cover how and why in the "Extracting the ingredients' flavor" on page 117.

Don't worry about overcrowding the tray, seasoning the meat, or coating it with a fat or oil. It may feel weird breaking these rules of the traditional roasting technique, but remember our goal isn't to make perfectly roasted meat, but rather to maximize flavor with no concern for texture or presentation. In fact, we want to encourage the meat to stick to the bottom of the pan to create as much fond as possible. Place the meat into the hot oven and roast it until it is well browned and a good bit of caramelized (but not burnt) fond is stuck to the bottom of the tray. That should take 30-45 minutes, depending on the amount of meat you're roasting and the size of the tray. More meat and a smaller tray will take more time, less meat spread out on a larger tray will take less time.

Fond

Fond is a French term that translates to "foundation." In cooking, the term fond is used to describe the browned bits of food that stick to the bottom of a pan. It consists of proteins, carbohydrates, and/or sugars that have caramelized via the Maillard reaction (defined on page 97), as well as any fats that may have rendered into the pan. These deposits are packed full of super-concentrated, rich, roast-y flavor, and are the foundation to any good pan sauce, as well as a major boost to your Thanksgiving stock. Fond is also commonly referred to as pan drippings when associated with making gravy for a roast.

Around 10 minutes before the meat is finished roasting, sauté the vegetables over medium-high heat using neutral oil. Add a pinch of salt to the vegetables. While stock is typically completely unseasoned, a conservative pinch on the vegetables will help extract their moisture and flavor without much risk of over-seasoning. The vegetables are ready when the moisture has cooked off and they have taken on some color.

Even though we've used two distinct techniques for the meat and vegetables—roasting and sautéing, respectively—they've both served the same two purposes: evaporating moisture and adding color. By evaporating water from the ingredients, we are concentrating the density of the flavor, while adding color through the Maillard reaction, which makes the flavor more intense, lending it a powerful punch of umami.

Deglazing the pan

Once the meat is roasted and the vegetables are sautéed, use a good pair of tongs to move the meat into the stock along with the vegetables. Add enough water to barely cover everything, then heat the stock just to a boil before reducing to a simmer. Meanwhile, fill the tray you used to roast the meat with around an inch of water and bring that to a boil. As the water in the tray boils, use a flat-bottomed wooden spoon to scrape up all the fond that has stuck to the bottom of the tray. You'll notice that as the fond is scraped off and mixed into the water, it will take on a deep brown color. This technique is called deglazing. Once you are confident that all the fond has been scraped up, pour the contents of the tray—the jus—into the stockpot. At this point, go ahead and add the herbs and spices and give it all a good stir to incorporate everything.

Extracting the ingredients' flavor

Continue to simmer the stock for at least three hours, but feel free to cook it for longer. If you decide to let it go for a prolonged period, make sure there is plenty of liquid, and put a lid on it to prevent too much evaporation, which would leave the ingredients dry enough to scorch and burn. As the stock simmers, foam may rise to the top. This foam will have collected impurities from the ingredients, so you should skim it off with a spoon or ladle and discard it.

After the stock has simmered for a sufficient amount of time, you must strain the liquid. I like to use a pair of tongs to pick out as much as I can (especially the larger bones) before pouring the stock through a mesh sieve over another pot or a large bowl. I know it can be tempting to taste the meat when you remove it. While it may look delicious, trust me, it's not. Remember, our goal was to extract all the flavor from the meat, so if we were successful, it should be very bland by now. If you don't want it to completely go to waste, the bland flavor won't stop your dogs from enjoying it. George and Wiley have even begun to develop a bit of a Pavlovian response to the smell of stock being strained! Just be very careful to make sure there are no small bones or bone fragments in any bits you give dogs or cats as a treat. Poultry bones can easily get stuck in their throats and lead to serious injury.

Last, remove the fat from the stock, which separates and rises to the top. The easiest way to do this is using a fat separator, a pitcher specially designed to help de-fat liquids. If you don't have one, use a spoon or ladle to skim off the fat. If you've made the stock ahead of time, you can refrigerate it and remove the fat easily once it has cooled and solidified. The stock will last for about 4 days in the refrigerator, but it also freezes very well.

Storage tip

If you are short on storage space in your fridge or freezer, or have an issue with the size of your containers, you can reduce the stock down to a smaller volume by simmering it uncovered. Just remember that your stock will then be concentrated, so you may want to dilute it with some water before using it if it's too strong or thick.

117

Gravy

On Thanksgiving, the sauce is boss. It mingles with the mashed, lingers on the turkey, and saunters with the stuffing. It compliments every flavor on the plate while uniting all of its components, ultimately resulting in a meal worthy of its own holiday. A good gravy balances a perfect texture with rich flavors and a deep color. Too thin and Thanksgiving dinner becomes Thanksgiving soup, too thick and you end up with a gloopy, unappetizing mess.

Components

The foundation of the gravy is turkey stock

(see page 111). The stock will give the gravy its primary flavor and color, while the gelatin from the bones will help to give the body to achieve that perfect texture. In addition to the stock, we can add complexity to the flavor profile by using alcohols like wine or sherry, we can thicken the texture with starches like flour, and round out the flavors while adding a silky shine with fats like butter.

Using store-bought stock

The technique outlined above is designed for homemade stock, but if you didn't get around to making stock this year, you can still use the method with just a few adjustments. There are three main differences between homemade stock and its store-bought counterpart:

Store-bought stock is typically already salted

Store-bought stock doesn't have significant amounts of gelatin

Its flavor isn't as bold or rich

To address these issues, there are a few things you can do. Be careful how much you reduce the stock. It can become very salty very quickly. Use a little bit of extra flour and butter in your roux to help thicken the sauce to make up for the lack of gelatin. Be more generous with your add-ins (see "Other add-ins" page 124). Especially when making your base, feel free to use plenty of ingredients, and even throw in extra vegetables like onions, carrots, or celery. Use the pan drippings from your turkey for a huge boost of flavor (see "Addressing the use of pan drippings" page 122).

How much
gravy should you make?

Traditional wisdom suggests one-third to one-half cup of gravy per person.

To ensure there's plenty for leftovers, let's go with a half cup (God forbid there's no leftover gravy!). Because there's so much reduction, start with half a cup of stock per person, then add an extra cup overall to be safe, plus 1/8 cup of wine per person.

So, for a dinner for eight, use 5 cups stock and 1 cup wine. You can always adjust the volume by adding stock or water, or by reducing what you have, so don't stress out about having exact measurements.

First, roughly chop one or two shallots. Don't worry about a

perfect, fine chop, these will be strained out. Heat a small amount of butter in a wide pot over medium heat and add the shallots, sweating them out until they just become translucent, which will bring out their sweetness.

Next, add your wine and crank up the heat to bring it to a boil before taking it down to a high simmer. This will evaporate the alcohol but leave the wine flavor. Allow the liquid to reduce down to a syrup, with the sugars just barley beginning to caramelize. The wider your pan and the higher the heat, the more quickly this will happen. I recommend a wide pan to help it to reduce more quickly, with a moderate heat to provide room for error. If the heat is too high and you over-reduce and burn the sauce, it cannot be saved. You'll have to start over. Add 1-2 tbsp of dry sherry and let that cook off as well, once again bringing your reduction to a syrupy state. If you don't have any dry sherry on hand and don't want to invest in a bottle, this step can be omitted.

Now, add about a cup of stock. Once again, allow it to reduce until it is thick and syrupy.

Add the remaining stock and bring it back to a simmer. The base should have more body than when you began, but should still be liquid enough to run off the back of a spoon. Along with texture, this process will add more richness and a touch of sweetness to the sauce.

What wine should I use in the gravy?

Price range: While it would be excessive to use an expensive, special-occasion wine for the sauce, I recommend making a moderate investment in the wine you use to cook. The quality of the wine comes across in the finished product. The old adage is, "Never cook with a wine that you wouldn't drink." Typically, cheap wines tend to be overly sweet, which is not a quality you want passed on to the gravy.

Type of wine: For Thanksgiving gravy, I recommend using a white wine. An easy way to ensure a good fit is to use the same wine you plan to drink, if you are having white wine with your meal. This will allow the wine you're drinking to pair with the dinner by helping it mirror the flavor of your sauce.

Because the process of making the base and then the gravy takes some time, I like to start it on Thanksgiving morning, leaving the pot of base on a low burner on the back of my stove.

If, before you're ready to complete the gravy, you've reached the point where you're satisfied with the reduction before you're ready to complete the gravy, put a lid on the pot and turn off the heat. If this happens a long time before dinner, periodically bring the sauce back up to a boil at least once an hour before turning off the heat, to prevent it from cooling to a temperature that may cause food safety issues. If you've over-reduced the base and it is too rich or thick, just thin it out with some water. When you're ready to make the gravy, strain the shallots out of the base with a fine mesh sieve.

Addressing the use of pan drippings

Pan drippings are the caramelized bits of fond and turkey fat that drips down into the pan while the turkey roasts. The drippings are packed with flavor and are considered by many to be the secret to an elite sauce. If you made your own stock, you have already collected pan drippings when deglazing the pan that was used to roast the stock meat. That step was designed to reduce your workload in the precious time leading up to Thanksgiving dinner. If, however, you are using store-bought stock, the pan drippings become an absolute necessity at this stage. Here, you will want to use the same technique outlined on page 116 to deglaze the roasting pans. Add the jus to your base before straining the base and adding it to your roux. By the way, even when you have made your own stock, you can always double dip on the pan drippings.

The rest is gravy.

Making a gravy

Roux 101

A roux is the combination of fat and flour, usually in equal parts, cooked together and used to thicken a variety of sauces and gravies.

Different types of roux are named for their color. Roux that are cooked longer are darker, and roux that are cooked shorter are lighter. The lightest roux is a blond roux, which is flour and butter cooked just enough to melt the butter and start bubbling, with no color added. This often is associated with a béchamel. The longest cooked roux is called dark chocolate roux, which is flour and oil cooked for a very long time, taking on a deep, dark brown color. Dark roux is often associated with New Orleans cuisine like gumbo. Typically, the darker roux are made with high smoke point oils, while lighter roux are made with butter. However, a roux can be made with any fat you like. The less a roux is cooked, the more it will thicken a sauce, and the more a roux is cooked, the more flavor it will add to a sauce.

Make a roux

To thicken our base into a true gravy, we need to make a light brown roux.

- Using roughly 1 tbsp of butter for every cup of base, add the butter to a saucepan and melt it over medium-low heat.
- Once the butter melts and starts to foam, add an equal amount of flour. Whisk them together and stir constantly until the roux has taken on a light brown color. Aim for the color of a latte.
- Carefully pour the base liquid into the roux, a very little bit at a time, whisking constantly. The more vigorously you whisk and the more slowly you pour in the base, the less likely clumps are to form, resulting in a smooth gravy.
- Bring the gravy just up to a boil, then reduce it down to a simmer. The thickening power of flour is heat-activated, so don't worry that the gravy seems thin before you bring it up to temperature. If you are concerned that any clumps of dissolved flour may have formed, strain the gravy through a fine mesh sieve.

If your gravy is too thick, thin it out with more stock or water. If it is too thin, reduce it down at a high simmer, stirring frequently to prevent the bottom of the pan from scorching. If you want to speed up this process, use a wider pot.

Making adjustments

Now that the gravy has come together, it's time for the most important step—tasting the sauce and adjusting the seasoning.

If you used homemade stock, it is likely that the gravy will need a lot of salt. When you season the sauce, add in a conservative estimate of how much salt you think it needs. Stir well, let it simmer for about a minute to allow the salt to dissolve, then taste it. You can repeat this process as many times as necessary, so take your time—it's always easier to add more salt to an under-seasoned sauce than to fix an over-seasoned sauce. If your gravy has become over-seasoned, the only remedy is to dilute it either with unseasoned stock, water, or heavy cream…at which point it would become a cream sauce—not traditional for Thanksgiving, but definitely a tasty fix in an emergency.

In addition to salt, consider seasoning with acidity. I like to add around 1-3 tsp of red wine vinegar to the gravy. This is not enough to make the sauce vinegary, but it will increase the acidity, making the sauce taste brighter while accentuating its flavors. If you've diluted the gravy with cream to adjust for over-seasoning, do not add any vinegar, as it may make the cream curdle.

Other add-ins

To make this sauce your own, you may want to invite a few more of your favorite flavors to the party. The two best times to add something extra are when you're building the base and when you're seasoning the finished gravy. While building the base, you can add larger or more solid herbs, spices, or vegetables that will be strained out with the shallots. Use ingredients such as:

- Dried mushrooms like porcini or shiitake for a boost of umami
- Fresh herbs like bay leaves, thyme, rosemary, or sage
- Whole spices, peppercorns, or seeds

When seasoning the finished sauce, you can add in liquids and ingredients that won't negatively impact the texture of the gravy, such as:

- Freshly cracked black pepper or finely ground spices
- Salty umami-laden fermented sauces like soy, Worcestershire, or fish sauce
- Sauteed vegetables like mushrooms for a less traditional, but exceptionally tasty mushroom gravy

With any of these add-ins, I recommend minimalism. You only want to accent the gravy, not overpower it.

We are
thankful for ...
...delicious side dishes.

- **Let the Stuffing Begin!**
- **Mashed & Sweet Potatoes**
- **Green Bean Casserole & Roasted Brussel Sprouts**
- **Mac & Cheese**
- **Cranberry Sauce**

Let the stuffing begin!

Stuffing is perhaps my favorite Thanksgiving side—it really has it all. Along with the bread, stuffing can host virtually any ingredient from meats to vegetables, herbs, and seasonings. While pedantic purists will point out that this recipe is technically for a dressing, as it isn't cooked inside the turkey, we have found that the word stuffing is used colloquially whether it is cooked inside the turkey or not. This stuffing is baked in a casserole dish, which allows it to have a crispy top and a moist, custardy center.

There are three core components to a great stuffing:

- Bread, toasted to make croutons
- Custard made from stock
- Eggs to add moisture and consistency

Plus:

- Mix-ins, made up of whatever meats, vegetables, herbs, or spices you prefer

The bread

Good bread is the foundation of great stuffing. To pick the best bread, we have to consider flavor, texture, and shape. Regarding flavor, I like to avoid overpowering sourdoughs, while still choosing something that has some level of fermentation. Texturally, hardier breads work best, so avoid anything delicate like brioche. Choose loaves that are large and have plenty of crumb—i.e. the inside of the bread. Something long and skinny like a baguette will have too much crust relative to the crumb, so avoid those. A nice rustic boule, peasant loaf, or Italian loaf works best.

If you really want to go above and beyond, you can always bake your own bread to make sure you get exactly what you want. I like to use a long batch fermentation—at least 12 hours—and a relatively high hydration, similar to Jim Lahey's famous no-knead bread.

Once you have your bread, tear it apart by hand, creating uneven chunks. Each torn piece should be less than 1 inch, but they don't all have to be the same size. Toss the bread in some fat. Oil works well, clarified butter works better, duck fat works best. Lay it all out in a single layer on a cookie sheet or roasting tray. Put the tray in the oven at 350°F and toast the bread until you have golden brown croutons. Take them out of the oven once they are cooked to perfection and allow them to cool completely.

Turkey custard

In order to provide moisture and bind the stuffing together into a cohesive dish, we'll use a custardy mix of cold or room temperature turkey stock combined with eggs and a splash of milk. Use roughly one whole egg for every cup of stock. You can add a little extra richness by adding in an extra egg yolk or two, or by adding some whole milk. Combine all ingredients in a mixing bowl and whisk until well blended.

I like to take any finely chopped herbs I'm using for the stuffing and add them directly into the custard so they get evenly incorporated throughout. My favorites are fresh sage, rosemary, thyme, scallions, and parsley, as well as dried oregano and fennel seed. Your selection should be informed by the ingredients you choose for the mix-ins. Add any herbs, as well as salt and pepper, into the custard and stir to blend evenly.

You want to make sure you have at least enough custard to thoroughly coat all the croutons. If you prefer a looser, crispier stuffing, use less, and if you prefer a more custardy, bread pudding-like stuffing, use more. When your croutons and custard are ready, put the croutons into a large mixing bowl or directly into the casserole dish, pour the custard over them, then roll up your sleeves and mix with your hands until you are confident all of the croutons are well-coated. Mixing the croutons with the custard before adding the mix-ins will help ensure that all the croutons are properly soaked.

The mix-ins

As the custard and croutons combine to make the base of the stuffing, you can now think of it as the canvas onto which you paint your masterpiece. With virtually unlimited options, you can keep the stuffing simple and elegant, or you can get creative and go over the top. To make this abundance of opportunity a little less overwhelming, I'll break down what I consider to be the three best stuffing strategies.

The minimalist approach

An ode to simplicity, the minimalist approach keeps it straightforward by focusing primarily on herbs, along with maybe a little garlic. If you're taking the minimalist approach, you've probably already added everything you need directly into the custard. The minimalist approach typically works best with a crispier stuffing, so don't go overboard with the custard-to-crouton ratio. It's a great option to put a delicious dish on the table that will serve as an excellent supporting cast member for the turkey.

The focused approach

The focused approach centers around one primary ingredient, with limited other ingredients selected specifically to complement it. So, for example, you might choose to focus on pork sausage and decide to throw in a little bit of fennel, mushrooms, and granny smith apples. Or maybe you focus on wild boar sausage and add in a few cherries. You could also focus on a vegetable like mushrooms, complimenting them with shallots, herbs, and a splash of sherry. Even seafood can work well in the focused approach. In fact, if you want a stuffing rooted in the traditions of the earliest Thanksgivings in New England, you could focus on oysters and compliment them with clams, leeks, and a splash of sauvignon blanc. The key to the focused approach is considering complimentary flavor profiles and being disciplined and deliberate with your selection of ingredients. It is a great option for showing off your culinary prowess with a fancy-sounding and elegant-tasting stuffing.

The kitchen sink approach

The kitchen sink approach is the all out, no-holds-barred approach to stuffing that yields a dish that is a Thanksgiving side only in name. Kitchen sink stuffing could stand as a meal in its own right. It is the approach I grew up with and still use. For example, my stuffing this year featured red onion, white onion, green onion, carrot, celery, fennel, leek, cremini mushrooms, shiitake mushrooms, Italian sausage, pancetta, garlic, parsley, sage, thyme, rosemary, oregano, fennel seed, dry sherry, and unoaked chardonnay. This approach is for the people who, when asked, "Why?" reply, "Why not?" It's an excellent strategy for presenting your guests with a stuffing that cannot be described as anything short of epic.

Regardless of the strategy you choose, start by slicing and dicing your ingredients. The golden rule for deciding how to cut an ingredient is to envision your final product. If your vision is a more consistent stuffing with homogenous bites, you may want to dice everything finely, whereas a rustic vision with varying textures may be best achieved by chopping ingredients into larger, uneven chunks. I typically use a variety of techniques, roughly chopping mushrooms, finely dicing hard vegetables like onions, carrots, celery, and fennel, and very finely mincing leafy herbs, garlic, and shallots.

Once you've prepped all of the ingredients, pre-cook everything by sautéing them separately before adding to the stuffing. This helps develop and concentrate their flavor by cooking off moisture, and makes sure that any meat is cooked through to a safe temperature. Start by cooking any fatty meats you are using, like sausage or pancetta, then cook the vegetables in the fat that has rendered off the meat. Deglaze the pan with any alcohol you may be using, or alternatively a splash of stock or water, to make sure you aren't leaving any flavor behind in the pan. If you are using alcohol, it is important to make sure you cook it out and reduce it, to avoid any harsh flavors.

After cooking the add-in ingredients, allow them to cool completely, then mix them thoroughly with the custard-coated bread. Move the mixture to a greased casserole dish and let it rest in the refrigerator until you are ready to bake. The longer it rests, the more the flavors will meld, so this is a great dish to prepare on Tuesday or Wednesday. Just be sure to take the stuffing out of the fridge an hour before it goes into the oven to let it warm to room temperature. When you're ready to bake it, cover the stuffing with a tight-fitting lid or tinfoil, and put it in a 375°F oven for 30 minutes. Remove the lid and continue to bake until the top browns and the center is hot, around 10-15 minutes. At dinnertime, pull the stuffing from the oven and serve piping hot.

Mashed potatoes

It simply isn't Thanksgiving without gravy's best friend.

This particular version of America's favorite side dish is inspired in part by Joel Robuchon's famous pommes purée, widely accepted as the best mashed potatoes in the world. As such, this recipe aims for a smoother puree of potatoes than many traditionally rustic Thanksgiving mashes, and utilizes an infused cream to impart the flavors of garlic, herbs, and peppercorns.

The potatoes

While there is a wide array of available types of potatoes, they can be generally divided into two main categories:

- Waxy potatoes, such as Yukon gold
- Starchy ones like russets

For our purposes, the waxy varieties will provide more potato flavor while maintaining a better texture that isn't compromised by too much starch. Based on their wide availability and ease of use relative to smaller varietals, I recommend using Yukon gold potatoes. The Yukon gold has a nicely dense interior without too much moisture, and a solid, distinctly potato flavor.

Because this method adds a fair amount of fat to the potatoes—this is Thanksgiving, after all—they will increase significantly in volume while also being quite rich. Therefore, you will not need as many potatoes as you would normally use for a more traditional mashed potato recipe. One medium potato should be plenty for two people, while still allowing for leftovers. If possible, try to get potatoes of relatively similar sizes, to help them cook evenly. The smaller the potatoes, the faster they will cook through, but the more of them you have to puree, so there's a bit of a tradeoff between cooking time and effort.

The fats

To maximize the rich decadence of the mashed potatoes, we'll use a combination of butter and cream. The butter should be cold and cut into roughly ½-inch cubes. This will allow it to slowly melt into the potatoes while maintaining its emulsion, almost as if you were making a beurre monté.

The cream presents an excellent opportunity to bring new flavors to the party. It is a great vehicle into which you can infuse flavors. I like to infuse an excessive amount of crushed garlic—six or more cloves!—whole black peppercorns, and herbs like rosemary, thyme, and sage. Simply add all the ingredients to a small pot and cover with the cream. Gently heat the cream to just below a simmer, trying not to let it come to a boil, and hold it at that temperature for 5-10 minutes. Cut the heat and let the mixture sit until you are ready to use it, then strain out and discard all the solids. The aromas of the infused ingredients should be pleasantly pungent in the infused cream.

Further additions

If you're feeling particularly luxurious and want to work truffle into your Thanksgiving feast, I certainly wouldn't stop you. Simply shave the truffle over the top as a finishing garnish, or mix in grated truffle using a micro-plane just before serving. If you're feeling luxurious without wanting to spend an arm and a leg, do what I do and work in some truffle flavor by replacing some or all of the butter with truffle butter.

When presenting the dish, a pad of melty butter sitting atop the potatoes can make a nice, decadent garnish. A sprinkle of chives will give it color. Alternatively, scallions, parsley, or crispy fried garlic chips all make excellent garnishes. To make garlic chips, slice garlic very thin, fry over medium heat in oil until just starting to brown, then strain.

Cooking the mashed potatoes

The process of making mashed potatoes can be broken down into three main steps:

- Cooking the potatoes
- Pureeing the potatoes
- Emulsifying the fats into the potatoes

Place your potatoes, whole and unpeeled, into a pot and cover them with cold water. A nonstick pot works best if you plan on reusing the same pot later at the emulsification stage. Place the pot over medium heat and bring it to a high simmer. The potatoes are best cooked whole and unpeeled so the skin can protect the flesh from becoming waterlogged.

Starting with cold water and keeping the water at a simmer rather than a rolling boil will ensure the skin doesn't burst open. The added benefit is that potatoes are much easier to peel after they've been cooked.

Continue cooking the potatoes until a fork can pierce all the way to the center of the largest potato with almost no resistance.

You will have a much harder time pureeing the potatoes if they are undercooked, so it's best to err on the side of cooking them longer. The time it takes to cook through will vary depending on the size of the potatoes.

Once they are cooked through, strain out the water. Allow them to cool just enough for you to handle them without burning yourself. For the best texture, the potatoes should not be allowed to cool completely, so be ready to work quickly.

Pureeing the potatoes

The goal in pureeing potatoes for mashed potatoes is to break down the flesh as finely as possible. A finer mash will create more surface area, allowing more butter and cream to be emulsified into the dish, and breaking down the larger starch granules will provide a smoother, more pleasant texture.

There are a variety of ways to break down the flesh of the potatoes into a proper mash, and because many of them utilize specialty equipment, I will list a few options. They are in the order of what I most recommend to what I least recommend.

Using a food mill: This technique breaks down the potatoes into a fine puree with relatively little effort. Cut your potatoes in half and place them flesh side down in a food mill set to its finest setting. Crank the food mill to force the potato flesh through to puree it.

The disk of the food mill should be able to catch the skin of the potato, but if you don't want to clean potato skin out of your food mill, peeling the skins off the cooked potatoes before pureeing the flesh is easy—it should come right off if you pull at it with your fingers, or use a paring knife if it is still too hot to handle.

Using a fine mesh sieve: This technique produces a high-quality result equal to the food mill, but it requires a bit more elbow grease. Cut your cooked potatoes in half and place them flesh side down on a fine mesh sieve. Use a spatula, spoon, or bench scraper—silicone works best—to force the flesh through the sieve. When you're finished, scrape off any of the puree that is still sticking to the bottom of the sieve. Barrel sieves work best for this, but a splatter guard can make a cost-efficient makeshift replacement, and any standard fine mesh sieve will get the job done. The sieve should be able to catch the skin of the potato, but if you don't want to clean potato skin out of the mesh, peeling the skins off the cooked potatoes before pureeing the flesh is easy—it should come right off if you pull at it with your fingers, or use a paring knife if it is still too hot to handle.

Using a potato ricer: This technique is easier than the sieve technique but will not break down the potatoes as finely. Cut your cooked potatoes in half and place them flesh side down in the ricer. If it has multiple settings, use the finest one. Push the potatoes through the ricer to puree them. The disk of the ricer should be able to catch the skin, but if you don't want to clean potato skin out of your ricer, peeling them before pureeing the flesh is easy—the skin should come right off if you pull at it with your fingers, or use a paring knife if it is still too hot to handle.

Using a handheld potato masher: This technique is not recommended because it will not break the potatoes down into a fine enough puree to allow a significant amount of fat to be emulsified into it. It is, however, quite easy to do, and may be the most convenient if you have a potato masher lying around. It may also be preferred if you are aiming for a more rustic, chunky mashed potato. Peel the skin from the cooked potatoes—or leave some in if you want to be extra rustic—using your hands or a paring knife. The skin will come off easily. Place the peeled potatoes into a pot and break them up using the potato masher until they reach your desired consistency.

Emulsifying the fats into the potatoes

Return the pureed potatoes to the pot. Set the pot on the stove over a low heat. You should have the butter, infused cream, and a little bit of warm water by your side. Constantly stirring the potatoes with a silicone or wooden spatula, alternate slowly adding in butter and cream, a little bit at a time. As you stir, be sure to scrape the bottom and sides of the pot to evenly incorporate the fats. If the emulsion gets too tight or looks like it is at risk of breaking, remove the pot from the heat, add a splash of water, and vigorously stir until it has returned to the desired consistency. Continue adding butter and cream until you are satisfied with the texture and richness of the dish, then season with salt and freshly cracked white pepper to taste. White pepper is best because it maintains the clean, white presentation of the potatoes, but if you don't have white pepper and don't care about that, feel free to use black pepper. Pour the potatoes into a serving dish, garnish, and serve.

For best results, the potatoes should be served right away. However, given how hectic the precious time is right before Thanksgiving dinner is served, the potatoes can be made up to a day in advance and they will still be delicious. Store them in the fridge until you are ready to use them, then gently reheat them in a pot over low heat, stirring frequently. If they have tightened up while resting, loosen them by adding a little extra cream.

Sweet Potato Casserole

Sweet potato casserole is essentially mashed sweet potatoes topped with marshmallows, and probably the most uniquely Thanksgiving of all the side dishes. You'd be hard-pressed to find this polarizing yet all-American treat served on any other day of the year. Its sweet flavor profile contrasts brilliantly against all the savory aspects of the feast, earning it the right to sit on the Thanksgiving table.

Preparation

The base of the sweet potato casserole is essentially a sweet potato mash. As with mashed potatoes, we make our sweet potato mash in three main steps:

- **Cooking the sweet potatoes**
- **Pureeing the flesh**
- **Emulsifying in some fats**

The specifics of these steps, however, differ from the mashed potato recipe in order to take advantage of some of the delicious properties unique to the sweet potato, while ultimately presenting a more rustic dish than the elegant *pommes purée* version of mashed potatoes.

Cooking the sweet potatoes

Sometimes, simplicity is best. This is one of those times. We're going to start off by making what, in my opinion, is the ultimate baked sweet potato. Place your sweet potatoes on a tinfoil-lined baking sheet and throw them into a 410°F oven. Don't poke holes in them, cut into them, or grease them or the tray. The goal here is to keep the skin intact, so it traps all the moisture inside the sweet potatoes. When that moisture turns into steam, pressure will build, and the internal temperature of the potato will rise high enough to caramelize the sugars inside the sweet potato. You're essentially creating a mini pressure cooker inside the sweet potato. You'll know you're finished when the jacket bursts, causing caramel to leak out of the potato onto the tray, and the skin caves in easily when you poke it. The exact time this takes will depend on your oven and the size of the sweet potatoes, but it should fall within the range of 45-75 minutes.

Pureeing the sweet potatoes

Sweet potatoes do not need to be pureed as finely as the Yukon golds used in the above mashed potato recipe. They do not have the same tough, large starch granules that need to be broken down. So, a handheld potato masher will work fine in this instance, though if you prefer to use a ricer or food mill, those work just as well. Remove the flesh from the skins of the sweet potatoes, either by scooping it out with a spoon or peeling away the skin with your fingers, then mash it up using your preferred tool.

Emulsifying fats into the potatoes

Sweet potatoes require much less fat than mashed potatoes—after all, they are going to be covered in marshmallows! Mix in a few knobs of cold butter, stirring constantly until the butter has fully melted into the sweet potato mash. Around 1-2 tbsp per potato should be plenty, depending on the size of your potatoes and how rich you want the mash to be.

Season the sweet potatoes to taste with salt. If you'd like, you can add warm spices like cinnamon or nutmeg as well, though I find that the flavor profile of the sweet potato, when caramelized with this technique, stands up quite well enough on its own.

The Marshmallow Technique

Once your mash is complete, scoop it into a casserole or pie dish. Use a spoon or spatula to level out the top of the mash to create a smooth surface for your marshmallow masterpiece. Now feel free to get as creative as you'd like! You can artfully arrange small marshmallows in patterns, throw in large marshmallows for variety, or scatter them randomly. I recommend making sure you cover the entire surface of the sweet potatoes, but how you do that is completely up to you. Once the marshmallows are all laid out, cover the casserole and put it in the refrigerator until you are ready to reheat it. The sweet potatoes are a great dish to knock out on Tuesday or Wednesday to make your Thanksgiving Day cooking a little less hectic. When you're ready to reheat the sweet potatoes, put them in a 350°F oven until they are warmed through and the marshmallow topping has browned.

The *marvelous* marshmallow mistake...

When I was making a batch of sweet potato casserole to test different techniques for this book, I made a mistake that opened my eyes to what may be the most delicious marshmallow topping I've ever had. I was trying to brown the marshmallows under the broiler when I was distracted for the few short seconds when marshmallows go from golden brown perfection to jet black burned. Not wanting to waste the whole dish, I peeled away the burnt top of the marshmallows, spread what was left of the molten marshmallow with the back of a greased spoon, then gave the dish a few seconds beneath the broiler to lightly brown the top. To our collective surprise, it was the most delicious of all our test batches!

Reflecting on the incident, I am reminded of making s'mores around the campfire as a kid. If you've ever been around a campfire making s'mores, you know there's always that one impatient, hungry kid who, not willing to wait for the perfect golden brown, employs the strategy of burning the marshmallow directly in the fire and peeling away the burnt husk. That kid then swears by his technique as not only being fast, but also the most delicious way to make a s'more. The rest of us, ignorant of their culinary genius, write this off as a cheap, messy technique...completely unaware of what we're missing.

Admittedly, emulating the marvelous marshmallow mistake may be a bit over-the-top, so here's how I would recommend doing it if you want to go the extra mile. Prepare and top the sweet potatoes as you normally would, then burn the marshmallows under the broiler. Peel away the burnt part of the marshmallows, then use the back of a well-greased spoon to spread what is left of the marshmallow evenly. If you're making the sweet potato casserole ahead of time, break here and refrigerate. Then on Thanksgiving Day, reheat the casserole in the oven as you normally would.

Green Bean Casserole

While green bean casserole is a traditional Thanksgiving dish, like sweet potato casserole, it can be polarizing. It can either awaken feelings of nostalgia and a celebration of tradition, or feelings of disgust toward a gloopy mess of canned ingredients. By using fresh ingredients we can resuscitate this dated dish, satisfying both nostalgic traditionalists and farm-to-table practitioners alike.

Green bean casserole consists of green beans smothered in cream of mushroom soup & topped with crispy fried onions or shallots.

The Green Beans

The first question we must address is which variety of green beans will best serve our casserole. Given that most varieties—string, snap, haricots verts—are more or less interchangeable in this recipe, it really depends on what is available fresh in your local market. If you're unsure what looks best, it's always safe to choose the French haricots verts. To prepare the beans, blanche them in a pot of salted boiling water until they begin to become tender. This should only take about a minute. Use a slotted spoon or a pair of tongs to remove the beans from the boiling water and immediately thrust them into ice water to prevent them from overcooking. Remove the beans from the ice water, pat them dry, and trim the tip and tail of the beans to remove the stems. You can either keep the green beans whole and long, or cut them into smaller segments. Once the green beans are prepared, add them into your casserole dish.

Cream of Mushroom Soup

As with the green beans, the first question to address is which variety of mushrooms will be best for the soup. And like the green beans, the answer really comes down to which mushrooms are the highest quality fresh at your local market. Personally, I think using multiple varieties can create a blend greater than the sum of its parts. I love mushrooms like cremini, shiitake, and oyster for this dish. In addition to fresh mushrooms, seasoning the soup with dried mushrooms can turn the flavor up to eleven. I like to buy dried porcinis and pulverize them in a food processor. The resulting powder, sometimes known as porcini dust, is an immensely flavorful and umami-packed seasoning that is perfect for cream of mushroom soup.

To prepare the mushrooms, brush off any visible dirt with a dry paper towel and roughly chop them into bite-sized pieces—half or quarter creminis, slice shiitakes, trim oysters off their stems. By brushing them clean rather than washing them, you're preventing the porous mushrooms from becoming waterlogged and washing away their flavor. If you find it absolutely necessary to wash the mushrooms using water, do so immediately before cooking.

Heat a stainless steel, cast iron, or carbon steel pan scorching hot over high heat, then add a generous glug of a high smoke point, neutral oil like grapeseed oil or vegetable oil, and throw in the mushrooms. Add salt immediately to coax out any water from within the mushrooms. Let that moisture cook off, then continue cooking the mushrooms over high heat until they are thoroughly browned. Add some diced alliums like garlic, leek, and/or onion, and a few sprigs of thyme. I find leek goes wonderfully with mushrooms. Turn the heat down to medium and continue cooking until the alliums are softened and slightly translucent. Deglaze the pan with a splash of brandy and continue cooking until all the liquid has evaporated. Pick out the thyme sprigs and discard, then set the vegetables aside while you prepare the base of the soup.

In a pot over medium low heat, start the base of the soup with a blond roux by combining equal parts butter and flour (for directions, see page 123). Roughly 1 tbsp of each per cup of liquid is a good place to start. So if you're using 2 cups stock and 1 cup cream, use 3 tbsp butter and 3 tbsp flour). Whisking constantly, add in turkey stock and turn the heat up to bring the soup to a boil before turning the heat back down to a simmer. Fold in the cream, then fold in the mushrooms. Season the soup with salt, pepper, and porcini dust to taste. This soup can be made a day or two ahead of time and reheated for the casserole on Thanksgiving Day. You can also make extra and have cream of mushroom soup for lunch on Tuesday or Wednesday, or freeze for a mid-winter treat. Once reheated, pour the soup over the green beans in the casserole dish when you are ready to serve.

140

Crispy fried shallots

One of the most genius aspects of a green bean casserole is the textural contrast that comes from the snappy green beans, the creamy soup, and the crispy fried topping. Start by peeling two or three shallots and slicing them into thin rings. Fill a pot ⅓ full with vegetable oil and heat it to 350°F. Lightly dredge the sliced shallots with flour by sprinkling flour over them and tossing to make sure they are evenly coated. Shake off any excess flour and very carefully drop the shallots into the oil. If you have to, work in batches to prevent overcrowding the oil. Once the shallots turn golden brown, remove them from the oil with a slotted spoon and drain them on paper towel. Season with salt immediately. The fried shallots are best when fresh but can be made a day or two ahead of time and stored in an airtight container. I also recommend that you make a little extra for two reasons: You might catch yourself snacking on them as you're cooking, and you may need backups if the first people to serve themselves monopolize the crispy topping. Add the shallots to garnish the casserole just before serving.

Roasted brussels sprouts

While brussels sprouts may not be as quintessentially Thanksgiving as turkey, stuffing, or gravy, they play an essential role in filling the green vegetable gap on Thanksgiving Day. No, green beans don't count when they're in a casserole covered with cream and fried shallots. Brussels sprouts are the perfect vegetable to play the part, because they are delicious, in season in November, and have enough to them to stand up to everything else going on at the overcrowded Thanksgiving buffet. Not to mention they are very "in" these days after being "out" for decades.

Preparing the brussels sprouts

- Preheat the oven to 400°F

- If purchased on a stalk, remove the brussels sprouts from the stalk and trim the stem of each sprout, then cut each sprout in half lengthwise.

- Place the prepped sprout-halves in a bowl—an over-sized bowl works best, making it easier to mix things into the sprouts. Toss the sprouts with a high smoke point oil like vegetable oil—save the extra-virgin olive oil for later. Season generously with salt and pepper.

- Lay all the sprouts on a roasting tray, cut side down. Set the bowl aside for later use.

- Place the tray in the pre-heated oven. Roast the sprouts until they begin to brown, roughly 20 minutes.
- Take the sprouts out of the oven and return them to the bowl. Toss them with balsamic vinegar and a little bit of extra virgin olive oil. If you want to add a touch of crushed red pepper flakes for a bit of a kick, add them now. I also like to mix in a few cloves of thinly sliced garlic.

- Return the sprouts to the roasting tray and put it back in the oven until the balsamic vinegar starts to caramelize and the sprouts are crispy, about 5-10 minutes. Be careful not to let the vinegar, garlic, or stray leaves from the sprouts burn, as they will turn bitter.

- Place the sprouts in a serving dish and serve.

Adding bacon

Whether you use bacon, pancetta, or guanciale, cured fatty pork makes an excellent addition to brussels sprouts. It is my opinion, however, that it is an unnecessary addition on Thanksgiving because of everything else going on.

That being said, who am I to tell anyone to shy away from bacon? If you feel like you just can't have brussels sprouts without it, here's the best way to add it in.

First cut the bacon, pancetta, or guanciale into small lardons (strips or cubes). Then blanch the meat by submerging it into boiling water for around 60 seconds. Blanching will remove any leftover salts or sugars from the curing process that would burn or cook unevenly when roasting with the sprouts, while also removing some of the smokiness that may otherwise be overpowering. Add the meat to the sprouts before roasting.

Did you know?

Until Lincoln made it a national holiday, the president needed to declare the Thanksgiving holiday each year. Jefferson refused to do so because he believed so firmly in the separation of church and state. Since the celebration involved prayer and reflection, he thought designating it a holiday was unconstitutional.

Macaroni & Cheese

I t's likely that you fall into one of two categories: you're either confused as to why mac & cheese is featured in a Thanksgiving book, or you're surprised I am qualifying why mac & cheese is in a Thanksgiving book. My mother made the analogy that serving mac & cheese at Thanksgiving is like watching Die Hard at Christmas. Everyone loves Die Hard, but its status as a Christmas movie is a hotly debated, polarizing subject. Whether or not you consider mac & cheese to qualify as a Thanksgiving side dish likely depends on where you are from. If you have roots in the deep South you are more likely to serve the deliciously cheesy casserole alongside your turkey.

While, in my family, we opt out of serving mac & cheese on our favorite Thursday, I decided to include this recipe in the interest of inclusivity and cheesiness. It can also provide reference for year-round comfort food even if you don't pair it with turkey.

The Sauce

The last few years

have seen an emergence of alternative techniques for mac & cheese, like the modernist approach of using sodium citrate to maintain the cheese's emulsion while melting it to create a pure cheese sauce that needs no added starches or bases (I've heard this referred to as 'science mac'), or the internet phenomenon of one-pot mac & cheeses, which typically rely on the starch from the raw pasta to act as a binder, while often including softer cheeses like cottage or brie. While these innovative approaches can provide a bit of convenience or a cool lesson in the science of emulsions, nothing can beat the traditional Mornay sauce-based mac because of its richness and depth of flavor.

—

Mornay Sauce

What is Mornay sauce?

Simply put, Mornay is a French sauce made up of béchamel with cheese, which begs the question: what is béchamel? A staple in French cuisine, béchamel sauce is one of the five French mother sauces and is made up of a blond roux and milk (a roux in this case is made of butter and flour, but for more on roux, check out the Roux 101 section in the Gravy chapter on pg 123). It is often seasoned with a touch of nutmeg. So, a bit of culinary algebra gives us the equation:

$$Mornay = (Béchemel + cheese)$$

$$Béchemel = (milk + roux), Roux = (butter + flour)$$

$$Mornay = (milk + butter + flour + cheese)$$

Traditionally in France,

Mornay is made primarily with gruyere, but for our mac & cheese purposes, we're going to use a cheddar base and compliment that with a blend of different cheeses.

144

Béchamel

A béchamel begins with a blond roux. Gently heat some butter (I typically use around 3 tablespoons for every pound of pasta) in a saucepan. Once it is melted, add an equal amount of flour, and whisk to incorporate. Just as the roux starts to bubble (before it has taken on any color), pour in whole milk while whisking constantly, and turn up the heat. I typically add around 3 cups of milk for every pound of pasta, but the best way to do this is by feel, rather than measurement. The sauce should become quite thin as you add the milk, then thicken a good bit once it reaches a boil. Reduce the heat down low, just below a simmer. If the sauce seems too thick, add more milk, and whisk to combine. It should be thinner than a typical béchamel, because it will thicken when the cheeses are melted in. At this point add a pinch of nutmeg (freshly grated, if possible) and a teaspoon or two of mustard. The flavor enzymes will mostly cook out, removing the mustardy flavor, but its emulsifying properties will remain, helping to maintain the creaminess of the sauce. Season to taste with salt, and if you'd like, feel free to add any other of your favorite spices here, like cayenne pepper or granulated garlic, or leave it as is, keeping the focus on the cheese.

Cheese

There are two things to consider when choosing cheeses for your mac: texture and flavor. By using a variety of cheeses, you can harness each of their unique advantages to maximize your success regarding both of those considerations.

There are a couple of ground rules that you should keep in the back of your mind. First, try to buy cheeses whole and grate them yourself rather than buying pre-grated cheese, which is often covered in a powder (like potato starch) to keep it from sticking to itself. Those additives can be problematic for the texture of your sauce. Also, avoid cheeses that are aged for eighteen months or longer. Not only do I think you miss some of the value of such an expensive cheese by melting it, but the crystallized protein structures of older cheeses may make your sauce grainy.

Texture-Benefiting Cheeses

I always like to include a little bit of processed cheese to help contribute to the creaminess of the sauce. All you need is a knob of Velveeta or a slice or two of American cheese. These cheeses are often processed with emulsifiers like sodium citrate. I also like to include a bit of mozzarella cheese, which has a stringiness to it that can give you sexy cheese-pulls, just like the hot, melty cheeses you see in commercials and influencers' Instagrams. Low moisture mozzarella is best here, as the fresh stuff doesn't melt as well and might add a little too much water to your sauce.

Flavor-Benefiting Cheeses

The selection of flavor-benefiting cheeses is a great place to make mac & cheese your own by choosing your favorite cheeses. For a traditional mac, sharp cheddar is king. Fifty percent of the total cheese I'm adding to the sauce is typically sharp cheddar, and I compliment that with ten percent texture-benefiting cheese (like mozzarella and American). That leaves forty percent open for creativity. Some of my favorites are gruyere, gouda, Jarlsberg, and Emmenthaler.

While that formula works well for me, don't feel locked into it. Designing your own cheese blend is a fun way to add personality and creativity to the dish, and let's face it, as long as you're serving pasta covered in gooey, melty cheese, it's going to be delicious!

Once you've shredded your cheese blend and made your béchamel, it's time to combine the two into a Mornay. Starting with your texture-benefiting cheeses, then moving to your flavor-benefiting cheeses, add the cheese in, one handful at a time, stirring until the cheese is nearly all melted before adding the next handful. By the time you're finished, the sauce should be very thick, and lifting your whisk out of the pot should create a long cheese pull.

The Pasta

The first half of the name "macaroni and cheese" is, well, macaroni. While macaroni emerged as the dominant pasta shape used in the cheesy casserole sometime in the late 18th century, the evolution of the dish since then has provided for a good deal of wiggle room. Rigatoni, conchiglie (shells), rotelle (wheels), and fusilli are all great alternatives. Or, if you believe in the adage "If it ain't broke, don't try to fix it," stick with the classic macaroni. Generally speaking, short, extruded pastas are best for this.

Mac & cheese calls for store-bought pasta, so feel free to leave your pasta machine in the cupboard.

The richness of an egg-based pasta is unnecessary given the richness of the sauce, so the semolina flour and water doughs that are typically used for boxed pastas are ideal. Additionally, the shorter cook time of fresh pasta can be problematic when trying to maintain an al-dente bite through the process of baking the casserole.

Bring a pot of water to a boil and salt it until it is roughly as salty as sea water. Add in the pasta and cook it for about ½ to ⅔ the time that the package recommends for al-dente, before straining out the water. The pasta should have softened up enough to be malleable, but not be cooked through.

The Topping

How could anyone improve on pasta covered a deliciously creamy, melty cheese sauce? With a crunchy topping of course! Fancy, gastro-pub skillet mac & cheeses will often feature a crispy, golden-brown crust of butter, cheese, and breadcrumbs that elevates the dish to new heights. But what if I told you there's a better way? Crushed up Ritz crackers (or any other butter cracker) can give you the crispiness of breadcrumbs with the buttery-ness built right in! You can pulverize them until they're the coarseness of panko for a more refined toping, just barely break them up for something more rustic, or mix it up and have a variety of brokenness to provide an array of textures. I like to mix my crushed up Ritz crackers with a handful of my cheese blend as well as some finely grated parmesan for the ultimate mac & cheese crispy topping.

Assembly

Thoroughly combine your cooked pasta and Mornay sauce in a buttered casserole dish before sprinkling the crispy topping all over it.

Cover the casserole tightly with tinfoil (if the casserole is very full, you may wish to grease the bottom of the foil with cooking spray to prevent any of your topping from sticking to the foil). This step can be completed the day before thanksgiving, and the casserole can be left in the fridge overnight. If you have refrigerated the casserole, take it out one hour before you're ready to throw it into the oven, to let it temper.

When you're ready to bake, put the casserole on top of a kitchen towel in a large tray. Fill the outer tray with boiling-hot water, enough to rise about halfway up the walls of the casserole dish, then slide the whole setup into an oven preheated to 375°F. This technique, which is borrowed from making the custard for a crème brûlée, will heat the sides and center of the mac & cheese more gently, resulting in a creamier finished product. After 10 to 15 minutes, remove the foil and continue to bake until the top has thoroughly browned (about another 10 to 15 minutes). Take the whole setup out of the oven, carefully remove the casserole from the tray, and serve hot.

Cranberry Sauce

Cranberry sauce is essentially cranberries cooked in a syrup. Thus, the first step is to make a simple syrup. Combine equal parts sugar and water in a pot and bring to a boil to dissolve the sugar. If you want to get creative, replace part or all of the water with something else, like orange juice. For the sauce, you want roughly a 1:1:4 ratio of sugar to liquid to cranberries. Reduce the heat to a simmer and add the cranberries. Season the sauce with a small pinch of salt. At this point, you may opt to be creative by adding an orange peel or orange zest, rosemary, star anise, cinnamon, nutmeg, or any other spices you'd like to use, to elevate the sauce. Cook until the cranberries burst and the liquid has reduced enough to form a cohesive sauce. As it cooks, the pectin will release from the cranberries, helping to bring body to the sauce. Remove any solid spices or zests you may have added, and pour the sauce into a serving dish. Cranberry sauce is best when made a day or two ahead of time.

We would be remiss if we did not recognize how important a particular type of cranberry sauce is to some families or family members. It is the kind that comes jellied in a can. I am hesitant to confess that we do not do Thanksgiving without it. In fact, in our research for the book, we found we are not alone. A whopping 86percent of our Instagram followers (@thegobblebook) shared that it is a staple on their Thanksgiving table as well.

We are thankful for...

...pies.

- Crust
- Apple
- Pecan
- Pumpkin

Pie Crust

Making your own pie crust is surprisingly easy, exceptionally delicious, and will leave your guests thoroughly impressed. This recipe is a sort of hybrid between a *pâte brisée* (pie crust) and *pâte feuilletée* (puff pastry), where the concept of folding the pastry to create beautiful layers is borrowed from puff pastry and applied to pie crust. The technique used for incorporating the butter into the flour may also be familiar if you've made homemade biscuits.

The ideal pie crust should be
crispy, flaky, and buttery.

To achieve these goals, as you fold the dough over itself to create layers, make sure the butter is cold throughout the process. If you live somewhere where it gets cold by the time November rolls around, it should be easy to keep everything cold. Otherwise, make sure to be extra diligent about chilling ingredients in the refrigerator between steps. With simplicity in mind, this recipe requires only butter, flour, water, and a pinch of salt. If you'd like to add a pinch of sugar for a sweeter dough, that's perfectly fine. I also recommend scaling the recipe up to make dough for multiple pies at once. Not only does extra dough freeze very well, but working with more dough makes it easier to get more layers when folding.

This pie crust can be used to make any pie, from your Thanksgiving desserts like apple or pecan pie, to a savory turkey pot pie with your leftovers.

Directions:

1   *Start with equal amounts of flour and butter—* that is, equal by *weight*, around 100 grams of each for one single-crusted pie. Season the flour with a pinch of salt and an optional pinch of sugar. Refrigerate the butter, flour, and bowl until all are well chilled.

2   *When everything is cold,* cut the butter into roughly ½-inch cubes. Toss the butter in the flour until it is well coated, then using your hands, pick up each cube and pinch it flat before returning it to the flour. If the ingredients have warmed up at all, return them to the refrigerator again to chill.

3   *Mix in just enough ice water to form a dough,* kneading it gently to encourage it to come together without aggressively forming gluten. It should come out to being roughly 50percent hydration, i.e. 50 grams of water for every 100 grams of flour. Once you make it a few times you'll be able to go by the feel without needing to measure. If the dough warms during this process, return it to the refrigerator to chill again.

4   *Roll the dough out into a flat rectangle until it is around ¼-inch thick.* Fold it over itself by bringing the two short ends together in the middle of the rectangle. Then turn it 90 degrees and fold again, bringing the ends of the other two sides together in the middle. If possible, fold once more, just folding it in half this time. The dough should now be several layers thick. Roll lightly over the top if necessary to even it out so it is still a rectangle or square.

5   *Portion the dough by cutting it into amounts appropriate for an individual crust.* Wrap them each tightly in plastic wrap, then refrigerate or freeze until you're ready to use them.

Apple Pie

This all-American dessert is an absolute must-have on Thanksgiving Day. A great apple pie filling is sticky and sweet with notes of warm spices like cinnamon and nutmeg, vanilla, and even a splash of bourbon.

The apples

When deciding on the variety of apple for your pie, consider how sweet or tart it is, how acidic it is, and how its texture is affected when cooked. Here are some of the best apples to consider.

Granny Smith

Granny Smiths are my favorite baking apples. They are the gold standard for most chefs. They lie firmly on the tart end of the spectrum, have a lot of acidity, and maintain their structure when baked.

Honeycrisp

Honeycrisp apples are super sweet, and baking them coaxes out that sweetness into a brilliantly complex and delicious flavor profile. They also do a good job of maintaining their structure when baked.

Braeburn

If you can get your hands on fresh Braeburns, they can't be beat. They have an amazingly strong apple flavor, a well-balanced level of sweetness, tons of flavorful juice, and a high degree of structural integrity. Just be careful of some of the less-than-fresh supermarket Braeburns—their quality can be inconsistent.

McIntosh

While McIntosh apples are slightly tart at the beginning of the season, they're much sweeter by the time Thanksgiving rolls around. McIntosh apples have an exceptionally distinctive flavor profile that can play well with fall spices. The soft flesh will not maintain its structure when cooked.

Sometimes, the best apple pies are made from a blend of apples. By combining apples with different flavors or textures, you can strike a balance better than the sum of its parts. Whatever apples you choose, keep their flavor profile in mind when designing the rest of the filling. If you chose Granny Smith, for example, you might cut back a little on the lemon juice to adjust for acidity, and be a little heavy-handed with the sugar, maple syrup, bourbon, or vanilla to adjust for sweetness.

Spices

Warm fall spices are your friends when it comes to apple pie, and cinnamon and allspice should be at the top of that list. Those two spices are fundamental to apple pie and will work well on their own, but for fun, compliment them with cardamom, nutmeg, clove, and/or ginger. Start with roughly three parts cinnamon to one part allspice, plus one part of any other spice you're using. Mix to combine, then taste a small pinch and adjust to your preferences. Don't worry if you end up with more than you need for this pie, you can save it and use it for all sorts of dishes that call for warm spices.

Sweetener

One of the keys to an excellent apple pie is building a complex base of sweetening ingredients. For this reason, we'll forgo overly simple sweeteners like white sugar, and think about using a combination of sweet ingredients. Lean on darker, richer sweeteners like light or dark brown sugar, as well as complex flavor profiles like vanilla extract or bourbon.

Other additions

- **Acidity**

  Adding the juice and the zest of a lemon can go a long way in brightening up the flavors of the pie and making them pop.

- **Salt**

  A pinch of salt will balance the sweetness a little bit while bringing out the flavors and making them more pronounced

- **Corn starch**

  A tablespoon or two of cornstarch will help to thicken the "sauce" of the filling and make it more cohesive.

- **Butter**

  A tablespoon of butter can help make the filling more luxurious and richer while taking the edge off of some of the acidity.

The Filling
Directions:

- To assemble the filling, combine all dry ingredients—sugar, spice, and cornstarch—and whisk together. Add both dry and wet ingredients together in a cooking pot, stir to combine, then add the apples to the pot and toss them in the mixture so they are well coated. Put the pot over medium heat and bring to a boil, stirring constantly until the mixture has reduced to a thick syrup. As it cooks, don't be afraid to taste and adjust the sweetness, acidity, spices, and seasoning. Just be very careful not to burn your mouth—the sugars in the filling can get very hot. When the syrup is thick, cut the heat and let the filling cool, then move it to the fridge and chill it for twenty minutes. Cooking the excess moisture out of the filling and chilling it before adding it to the crust helps to allow the bottom crust to be crisp.

- While the filling is cooling, roll out the bottom crust. It should be at least six inches larger than your pie dish in diameter and around ⅛-inch thick. Lay the dough into the pie plate, gently pressing it flush with the walls and any corners, then chill the dish and crust in the fridge for 5-10 minutes.

157

- Meanwhile, start preheating your oven to 425°F and place a cookie sheet on the middle rack. Prepare an egg wash by beating one egg with a couple teaspoons of water or milk. Roll out the dough for the top crust into a circle at least two inches larger than the pie dish in diameter, and roughly ⅛-inch thick. When the pie plate and filling are thoroughly chilled, brush a little egg wash around the edges of the pie where the bottom crust will meet the top crust. Pour the filling into the pie and lay the top crust over the pie. Trim away any excess crust, then flute or crimp the edges to seal the top and bottom crust together. Brush the top crust with egg wash and cut a few slits in it to allow steam to escape. Alternatively, decorate the top crust with fall patterns or designs using any excess dough, brushing each piece with egg wash, or decorate by sprinkling turbinado sugar over the top crust of the pie.

- Place the assembled pie in the freezer for twenty minutes to ensure it is thoroughly chilled, then move the pie directly from the freezer onto the hot sheet pan in the preheated oven. After around 10-15 minutes when the crust starts to brown, reduce the heat to 350°F and bake for another 30 minutes. Finally, turn the heat back up to 425°F and continue to bake until the crust is well browned. Remove the pie from the oven and let cool.

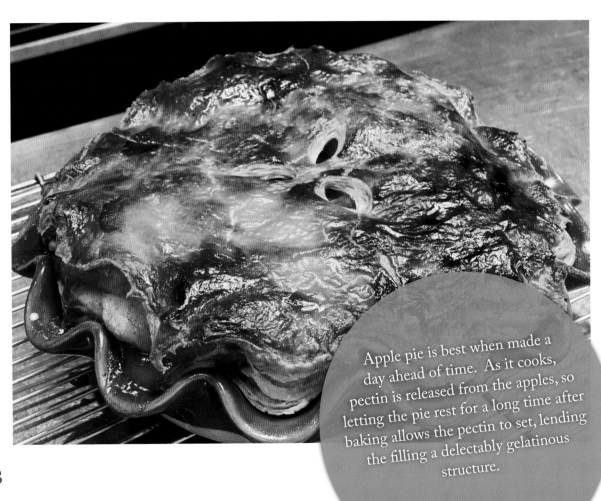

Apple pie is best when made a day ahead of time. As it cooks, pectin is released from the apples, so letting the pie rest for a long time after baking allows the pectin to set, lending the filling a delectably gelatinous structure.

Pecan Pie

Pecan pie, a Southern staple and Thanksgiving classic, is all about contrasts. It should be sweet but also salty, and ooey gooey in the center but crispy and crunchy on the surface. It's super easy to make from scratch, making it the perfect way to begin a new tradition of baking your Thanksgiving pies at home.

The core ingredients of pecan pie filling are:

- Pecans
- Sugar
- Corn syrup
- Butter
- Eggs

In addition to those five, the pie can be elevated with vanilla extract, bourbon, and a pinch of salt.

Pecans

For a standard 9-inch pie dish, use 2 cups of shelled pecans.

Sweeteners

You should aim for 2 cups total, split between sugar and corn syrup. A great place to start is 1 cup light corn syrup, ¾ cup white sugar, and ¼ cup light brown sugar, but feel free to play with the ratios to fit your taste. Just be sure to stay around 2 cups total.

Eggs

Use 3 large eggs. Beat them thoroughly with a whisk before combining with the other ingredients.

Butter

For the most luxurious and decadent pecan pie, use a full stick of unsalted butter, melted.

Other additions

These additional flavors have a little more wiggle room for you to adjust to personal preference.

Add:

- 1-2 tsp of vanilla extract
- 1-2 tbsp of bourbon (or omit the bourbon completely, if you prefer)
- 1-2 tsp salt

159

Pecan pie directions:

- Preheat your oven to 350°F with a sheet pan on the middle rack.

- Roll out the dough into a large circle, at least 6 inches larger in diameter than your pie dish and roughly ⅛-inch thick. Lay the dough into the dish, gently pressing it flush with the walls and corners. Trim the dough, then (optionally) crimp the top using your fingers to pinch and push the edges into a decorative pattern. Move it to the refrigerator to chill while you assemble the filling. This pie has no top crust.

- Combine all ingredients except the pecans in a mixing bowl, and whisk until homogenous. Add the pecans and stir until they are well coated. Pour the mix into the pie crust, then (optionally) decorate the pie by arranging a top layer of pecans in a decorative pattern or adorning the top with scraps of crust dough trimmed into decorative shapes. Put the pie in the oven, placing it onto the hot sheet pan.

- Bake the pie for 40-60 minutes, checking to see if it is done by giving it a little wiggle. The edges should be set, but the center of the pie should jiggle slightly. When the pie is done, remove it from the oven and let it cool completely. Pecan pie can be made up to three days ahead of serving if you keep it in the refrigerator.

Bring it up to room temperature or warm it slightly in the oven before serving.

Pumpkin Pie

It just isn't Thanksgiving without pumpkin pie.

This deliciously classic single-crusted pie stands out with its velvety smooth, well-balanced custard filling. The filling is made up of:

- Pumpkin puree
- Warm fall spices
- A sweetening element
- A dairy element
- Eggs

Pumpkin puree

Classically, the pumpkin element of a pumpkin pie comes out of a can. I recommend getting a can of unseasoned, unsweetened pumpkin puree, as that will allow you to control the quality and quantity of the spices and the sweetener that you use. Especially in the chaos of a pre-Thanksgiving kitchen, saving time, effort, and kitchen space by taking the canned route is a great way to free yourself up to invest in scratch-making something else that will have a greater effect on the finished product, such as the pie crust.

If, however, you insist on a farm-to-table, from-scratch version, there are a few things to keep in mind.

Not all pumpkins are created equal. The texture and flavor of different pumpkin varieties can vary greatly. For pie, you want a sweet pumpkin with drier, less fibrous flesh. Your best bet is going to be a sugar pumpkin, also known as a pie pumpkin.

Sometimes the best "pumpkin" isn't a pumpkin at all. As a stand-in for pumpkin, consider using alternative but similar vegetables, such as butternut squash, that have less moisture, smoother texture, and more flavor and sweetness. Sweet potatoes also add great flavor and provide a sturdier texture. The best "pumpkin" pie could have a balanced blend of pureed sugar pumpkin, butternut squash, and sweet potato as a filling. Start with a ratio of somewhere around 2:2:1 pumpkin to squash to sweet potato, and adjust to taste. If you do substitute some or all of the pumpkin for a sweeter alternative, be sure to adjust accordingly by cutting back on any added sweeteners like sugars or syrups.

Directions:

To puree the pumpkin or squash, cut it in half and roast it low and slow in an oven, flesh side down on a sheet pan, until its flesh is soft and has begun to caramelize. This will make it easier to puree, remove some of the excess moisture, and bring out the sugars while deepening their flavor through caramelization. Scoop out the flesh and puree in a blender until smooth. To puree a sweet potato, follow the steps outlined in the sweet potato casserole recipe on page 134.

Spices

Pumpkin spice—which gets its name via its association with pumpkin rather than having any pumpkin in it—makes up the true soul of a pumpkin pie…so much so that a butternut squash pie seasoned with pumpkin spice would be far more recognizable as a pumpkin pie than a pie using actual pumpkin filling but without the traditional spices. The core spices that define pumpkin spice are cinnamon, ginger, and clove. Most iterations will also include nutmeg and allspice to round out the flavor profile. By combining these ingredients yourself instead of buying a premade mix, you can control the ratios and optimize them to your personal taste. Just keep adding to the mix based on what you feel it needs more of, tasting a pinch as you go. Don't worry if you make too much, extra pumpkin spice is never a bad thing to have in your pantry!

Sweetener

While many traditional recipes call for it, white sugar is, frankly, boring. Add depth, richness, and caramel notes to your filling with sweeteners like brown sugar, demerara sugar, maple syrup, or even agave nectar. Similar to using a combination of vegetables in your filling, combining two or more sweetening elements can elevate the pie by adding complexity. You can also consider upping the flavor with a touch of vanilla extract.

Dairy

The key consideration when adding dairy to a pie is making sure you aren't adding too much moisture. That's why traditional recipes often call for evaporated milk. While evaporated milk works wonderfully, if you want to explore alternatives for a less traditional pie, consider things like cream cheese, sour cream, mascarpone, or *crème fraiche*, any of which will add a lot of richness without a ton of moisture, and will lend a cheesecake-like tang to the filling.

If you really want to kick the richness up to eleven, consider adding a tablespoon or two of melted butter into your mix.

Eggs

Eggs are critical to obtaining the perfect custardy texture in your filling. Two large eggs is the standard for one pie. Crack the eggs into a mixing bowl, season with salt, then whisk them on their own before adding any other ingredients. The salt will help break down the eggs, and whisking them will ensure the yolks and whites fully homogenize.

Pumpkin pie directions:

Add all of the filling ingredients to the beaten eggs and stir to combine until smooth and homogenous. Pass the filling through a fine mesh sieve to ensure an especially smooth, silky, and luxurious pie. For best results, assemble the filling ahead of time and let it sit overnight. This allows the flavor of the spices to really blossom and meld with the other ingredients.

To ensure a crispy crust, use a technique called a partial blind bake. This means baking the pie crust partially before adding the filling and baking again. First, roll out the dough into a large circle at least 6 inches larger in diameter than your pie plate and roughly ⅛-inch thick. Lay the dough into the dish, gently pressing it flush with the walls and any corners. Trim the dough, then (optionally) crimp the top using your fingers to pinch and push the edges into a decorative fluted pattern. In order to prevent the flaky crust from puffing up on the bottom and shrinking down on the sides (which would leave little to no room for the filling), it needs to be weighted down. Put a piece of parchment paper over the crust and place pie weights over it. If you don't happen to have pie weights in the cupboard, dried beans will make a great substitute.

When the pie crust is all set to go, put it in the freezer for 15-20 minutes to get it nice and cold. Preheat the oven to 400°F and place a sheet pan onto the middle rack. Move the cold pie plate and crust directly from the freezer into the oven on the hot cookie sheet. Bake until the edges start to brown, around 10-15 minutes.

Remove the dish from the oven and carefully lift the parchment paper along with the weights out of the crust. Dock the crust by poking holes all over the bottom with a fork, then return the pie to the oven until the bottom is browned, around 6-7 minutes. Docking the crust allows steam to escape, helping to prevent the bottom from puffing up. This technique of double-blind baking helps to make the pie crust super crispy and delicious without losing its shape.

When browned, remove the crust from the oven and reduce the heat to 300°F. Pour in the filling and return the pie to the oven, baking it for 35-45 minutes, or until the center is set. Cooking the custardy filling low and slow helps to keep it silky and delicious.

We are
thankful for
...leftovers.

by Christopher

- **The Quintessential Thanksgiving Sandwich**

- **Turkey Tet 2.0**

- **Turkey Pot Pie**

Thanks Again!

The leftovers

By definition, Thanksgiving means cooking in excess.

This celebration of abundance provides a wonderful opportunity to get creative and repurpose leftovers into their own delicious, unique meals.
Here are three of my favorite ways to utilize Thanksgiving leftovers.

The Quintessential Thanksgiving Sandwich

Perhaps the most iconic of all leftovers is the Thanksgiving sandwich, where one is given annual permission to stuff a full meal in between two slices of bread for Friday's lunch.

A leftover-filled sandwich is best served hot, so the first step is reheating your leftovers. A microwave works fine for this. If you are the bread-toasted type, heat a pad of butter in a nonstick skillet over medium heat, place two slices of your favorite bread in the pan—I like a rustic sourdough—and toast them until perfectly golden brown. Remove the bread from the pan and spread each slice with a generous helping of cranberry aioli, which you can make by mixing equal parts mayonnaise and leftover cranberry sauce.

Begin building the sandwich with your cold ingredients, greens first. Arugula is ideal, but any other leafy green works. Cold ingredients should always go on the bottom of a hot sandwich to keep them protected as the heat rises. Next, layer on the stuffing, then some relatively thin slices of turkey breast, followed by a spoonful of mashed potatoes. Sandwiching (yes, pun intended) a solid ingredient like turkey between two softer ingredients will help maintain the structure, and using white meat will provide the best texture. If you really want to be decadent—and with a sandwich like this, who doesn't?—fry up a piece of turkey skin in the pan you used to toast the bread, and place that on top of the potatoes. Finally, top the sandwich with the other slice of bread and, when you're ready, transfer it to a plate, cut it in half, take a picture of the ridiculously awesome cross section, and post it on Instagram. Don't forget to tag us @thegobblebook! Serve with hot leftover gravy for dipping, and consume with extra napkins handy.

PK's recommended
Thanksgiving sandwich wine pairing:
Chinon

For this recommendation, I went no further than Vanessa Price, author of *Big Macs & Burgundy*—a must read for wine enthusiasts. Regarding chinon, Vanessa points out, "The loudest flavor in the Thanksgiving leftover sandwich is cranberry sauce, so you want a wine with enough acid to play along with that trumpet. Chinon also has enough fruit and structure to buttress the gravy and mayo." Coming from the Loire Valley, this wine is made from cabernet franc, which imparts vegetal flavors and fairly high acidity. Leave it to Vanessa to nail the perfect match.

Thanks, Vanessa!

Turkey Pot Pie

This deliciously nostalgic, double-crusted savory pie is a perfect use for leftover turkey, gravy, and piecrust dough. If you don't have enough leftover gravy, you can whip up a fresh, simplified batch using leftover stock. Follow the instructions on page 132 to make a light brown roux, then whisk in the stock.

Ingredients and directions:

Filling

Start by dicing up some vegetables like onions, carrots, celery, and mushrooms, and sweating them out in a pan over medium heat. In the spirit of cooking with leftovers, feel free to substitute or add to the listed vegetables with whatever you have lying around.

Once the vegetables have softened and some of the moisture has cooked out, add in your leftover gravy. If cold, it will likely be solid from the gelatin in the stock, but don't worry, it will melt in the pan. Once the gravy has melted, thin it a little with a splash of whole milk. Throw in some frozen peas and/or frozen corn if you have it, as well as some leftover turkey. Cook and stir the mixture until it is cohesive and slightly thickened. Transfer to a bowl and let it cool completely.

Crust

Using some leftover Thanksgiving pie crust dough for the bottom crust, roll it into a large circle, about ¼ inch thick. Lay the crust out over a lightly-floured pie dish or cast iron skillet, and gently press the dough to fit against the bottom and sides of the dish or skillet. Fill the crust with the chilled filling and move it to the refrigerator to keep cool.

Using some more leftover pie crust dough for the top crust, roll it out into a circle that is roughly ¼-inch thick. Grab the pie from the refrigerator and lay the top crust over it. Trim both layers of the crust to be even with the edge of the dish or skillet, then flute or crimp the edges together to seal them. Cut slits in the top crust in a decorative pattern to allow steam to escape. Brush the top crust with egg wash—an egg, beaten with a splash of milk—then chill the whole pie in the freezer for 10-20 minutes.

Preheat the oven to 425°F, then move the pie directly from the freezer onto a preheated sheet pan on the bottom rack of the hot oven. Bake until the crust starts to brown, around 5-10 minutes. You may have to rotate the pie occasionally to make sure the browning is even. Now turn the heat down to 350°F and continue to bake until the filling is hot and bubbly, which should take 25-30 minutes. Finally, crank the heat back up and bake the pot pie at 450°F for 5 more minutes, or until the crust is hot, browned, and crispy. Pull the pie from the oven and let it cool for at least 10 minutes before serving.

PKs recommended
pot pie wine pairing:
Chenin Blanc

It is time to revisit a bottle of nicely chilled chenin blanc. You'll likely want one that has seen some oak, so the wine can stand up to the creaminess of the pie.

Turkey
tet 2.0

Turkey tetrazzini, a creamy pasta casserole, is a longstanding leftover tradition in our family. It's so fundamental to our "thanks again" experience that it has even earned a colloquially shortened nickname: turkey tet. This recipe is called turkey tet 2.0 because it leverages the idea of a creamy turkey and mushroom pasta, but disposes of the more dated aspects like baking it in a casserole. After all, Thanksgiving Day has already had more than enough casseroles.

Ingredients and directions:

Start the sauce by sautéing some mushrooms over high heat until they are well browned. Reduce the heat and add some onions or whatever alliums you have lying around—leeks or shallots work great here. Continue cooking until the onions are soft and translucent. Throw in some thinly sliced garlic, dried oregano, and some red pepper flakes if you want a kick. Once the garlic becomes fragrant, add in some leftover turkey stock and heavy cream—just enough to make it a sauce. Bring the liquid to a simmer and let it reduce until it thickens slightly. Add shredded leftover turkey.

Meanwhile, cook ¼ pound of pasta per person in salted boiling water for 2 minutes less than the package directions for al dente. Any pasta will work, but long pastas that are a little wider, such as pappardelle or tagliatelle, work exceptionally well. Using tongs or a slotted spoon, transfer the pasta directly into the sauce, letting some of the pasta water come with it.

Vigorously stir the pasta with the sauce until the pasta is cooked through to a satisfactory al dente level, roughly 2 minutes, since you shortened the time the pasta cooked by 2 minutes. Mix in an excessive amount of freshly grated parmesan cheese and a handful of finely chopped parsley. Serve with hot, crusty bread, more freshly grated parmesan cheese, and red pepper flakes.

PKs recommended
turkey tetrazzini wine pairing: *Pinot Noir*

Pinot noir will hit the spot! Its light body and bright fruit notes contrast very nicely with the starchiness of a turkey tetrazzini. Not to mention, pinot noir and mushrooms are a match made in heaven!

We are
thankful for...

...Grace.

by Nadine

Say grace

Grace in our family has always been delegated to the youngest. I am not certain where this tradition came from. As I think about it now, it's probably a little sadistic.

What were we thinking?

Being in the presentation coaching business, I know that one of the greatest fears for many people is public speaking. And here we were, asking a six- or seven-year-old child to lead a prayer of thanks with all his older cousins, aunts, uncles, and grandparents staring at him.

When Christopher was about fifteen, it occurred to him that he could hand off his grace-saying duties to his seven-year-old cousin, Annabel. He pulled a fast one. Moments before the meal, he announced the hand-off. All of the adults looked at poor Annabel, encouraging her. "Say grace, Annabel." "Say grace." "Annabel, say grace." We must have repeated it three or four times. Finally, a reticent Annabel looked up at all of us with her big blue eyes and said, "Grace." Served us right. Clearly we need to change this tradition. Apologies Jamie, Chris, and Annabel!

I grew up in a Catholic family where, like so many, we recited the traditional grace before every meal.

Bless us, oh Lord, and these Thy gifts which we are about to receive from Thy bounty, through Christ our Lord. Amen.

I must admit that often the goal was to see how fast one could get to the "Amen." Rarely did I really internalize the words that I, or any else, was saying. Through the years, however, its meaning and importance has grown for me. I must say, my preference is an impromptu, from the heart grace that speaks to the current situation by recognizing new and absent family members, specific blessings, and challenges.

This last Thanksgiving was especially grim without Peter, and our other family members unable to attend due to the Covid pandemic. Additionally, we were very aware that we were not alone. Hundreds of thousands of families were experiencing empty seats at the table for the first time, and many more were struggling to pay for the food at their table. Annabel, now 16, with no prompting this time, said one of the most beautiful graces I can remember. I guess those nine years of experience paid off.

Conducting research for this book, I wondered what alternatives there are to the traditional wording for grace, and we found a few to share with those of you who may want a quick, well-versed prayer in your back pocket.

Lord, thank You for the food before us, the family and friends beside us, and the love between us.

Thank you, God, for this food. For rest and home. And all things good. For wind and rain and sun above. But most of all, for those we love.

We thank You, Lord, for all You give. The food we eat, the lives we live. And to our loved ones far away, please send your blessings, Lord we pray. And help us all to live our days with thankful hearts and loving ways.

(from beliefnet.com)

We are
thankful for...

by Nadine

...Peaceful and Fun Family Gatherings

- Thanksgiving & Politics
- Planning & Discipline
- Questions Never to Ask

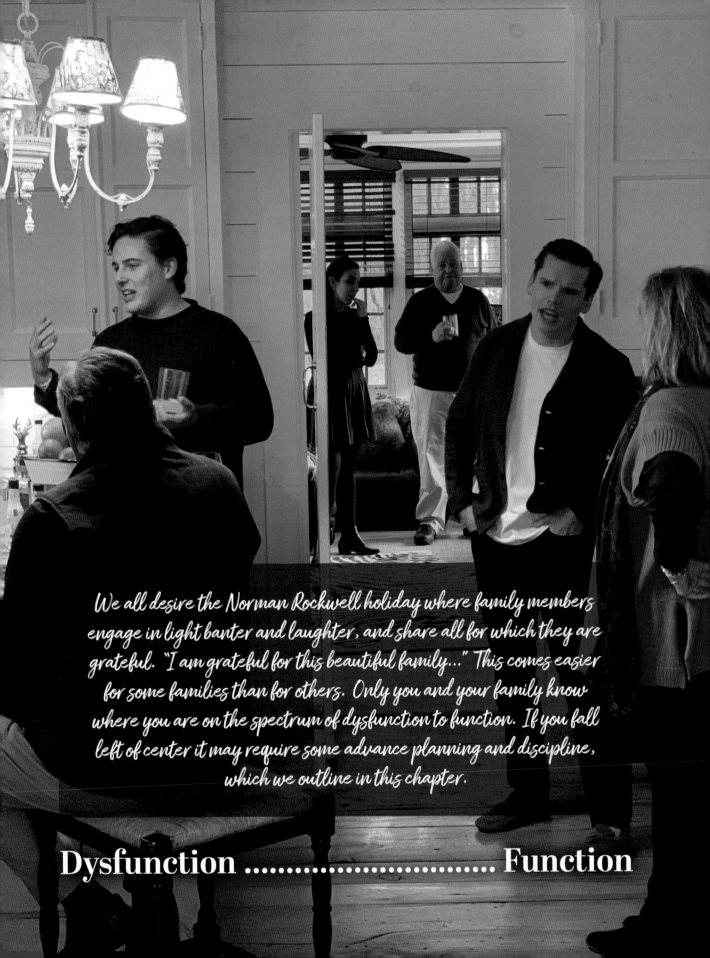

We all desire the Norman Rockwell holiday where family members engage in light banter and laughter, and share all for which they are grateful. "I am grateful for this beautiful family..." This comes easier for some families than for others. Only you and your family know where you are on the spectrum of dysfunction to function. If you fall left of center it may require some advance planning and discipline, which we outline in this chapter.

Dysfunction .... Function

Thanksgiving & Politics

The recent political environment has created a divisiveness we have not seen in modern history. I'm sure we have all heard stories of family and longtime friendships that have not been able to survive the differences in opinion that stem from the political unrest.

In 2018, Amy Janan Johnson, a professor of communication at the University of Oklahoma, published a study that documented the experiences of 479 college students who went home for Thanksgiving following the 2016 presidential election. In an article for FiveThirtyEight.com, Johnson shared some insight from her study.

She found that some families are "conversation oriented," where talking about controversial issues is normal, while other families are "conformity oriented," where touchy topics are off-limits and high value is placed on uniformity of thought. In a heated election environment like 2016, it was often impossible for the conformity-oriented families to avoid the subject of the election. When it raised its ugly head, they did not have the experience to deal with disagreement amicably.

Johnson also noted that there are serial disagreements that families carry on for years and never resolve. Some of these are personal, such as leaving the toilet seat up, and others are value-oriented, like climate change. As long as you argue productively by avoiding behaviors such as yelling and name-calling, you can argue about the same things every Thanksgiving and still maintain strong relationships within the family.

Her study also found that many people think of politics as an abstract issue, when, in fact, political issues are often proxies for personal values. One of the reasons it's hard to change people's minds on something like climate change is because the debate isn't really about the facts, but about deeply held personal values. This is when it can get messy around the holiday table. For that reason it is important to have perspective on those value-based beliefs, and be able to walk away when necessary, for the sake of the relationship.

The good news is that families who share basic values find it is easier to disagree about details without feeling hurt, and when family members' politics are in alignment, a tough political landscape can end up bringing them closer together.

When your family get-together requires some planning & discipline...

Determine in advance what subjects are off-limits

You may decide to communicate this before Thanksgiving, or agree in advance with your immediate family that if a certain subject comes up you will politely shut it down.

Make it all about them

If there is a family member with whom you have had a difficult history, think in advance about two or three questions you can ask that person. Is he a car buff? Ask what he thinks of the new Tesla. Is she a book lover? Ask her what was her favorite book of the year. When they answer, say, "Tell me more," and try to listen with genuine interest. The idea here is to set the tone. People love to talk about themselves and their interests, and it keeps the conversation off that time you told Mom and Dad that your cousin was smoking cigarettes behind the garage.

Compliment

Authentic compliments are always appreciated. Before the event, think about what you genuinely admire about each family member, and make a commitment to voice it. "We can always count on you for looking dapper,

Uncle Ed." "Cousin Suzie, I love how you always bring humor to our table."

Try to find similar interests

Funny stories about childhood, past vacations, or favorite television programs can ignite that forgotten connection. Who doesn't love to debate if the Partridge Family or the Brady Bunch was the better show?

Consider using a neutral ice-breaker at the dinner table

In my training programs, I often ask people to share a television program they are embarrassed to tell people they watch. Believe me, there are many of them. Think *My 600 Pound Life, Naked & Afraid, My Strange Addiction, Hoarders*, etc., etc. I had to look these up of course, as I personally only watch highly-cultured programs like *Housewives of New York* and *Southern Charm*.

Invite a new friend

For some families, it is easier to behave nicely if there is an outsider in the room. Invite a friend who may not otherwise have a place to go for the holiday.

Questions never to ask:

When are you two going to get engaged?

Do you have a boyfriend yet?

How's that job search going?

Oh my goodness, you are not going to have _another_ piece of pie, are you?

Where's that nice young man you brought *last* Thanksgiving?

We are thankful for ...
...An Easy Cleanup

by Nadine

- **Strategies & Tips**
- **Common Tasks to Delegate**

Some dread the turkey trot, others dread uncomfortable conversations, but one thing we all have in common is our dread of the most massive kitchen cleanup of the year. Even the simplest of menus include multiple side dishes that result in baked-on messes. You can count on there being a lot of fat involved—aka grease—and lots of dishes, glasses, serving trays, silverware, pans, etc. Add to this mayhem the enthusiastic consumption of cocktails, wine, plus a sleep-inducing meal and dessert, and you have the greatest challenge any holiday can offer. I'm exhausted just writing about it. Fortunately, with some organization, pro-tips, and the right frame of mind, the Thanksgiving cleanup doesn't have to be as Sisyphean as it seems.

My brother-in-law, Ray (you know him as "the Mista" if you follow my Sista's very popular blog, preppyemptynester.blogspot.com—and if you don't, you are missing out), attended the Culinary Institute of America. He manages hotels now, but his early CIA training is evident in everything he does. What has most impressed us over the years is that no matter what stage you find him in the cooking process, his kitchen is always as picture-perfect as his food. We try to channel Ray throughout Thanksgiving Day. Sometimes we are more successful than others, but we have definitely improved over the years. This is what we have learned so far.

Make tinfoil your friend

When I see tinfoil on a roasting pan, I immediately want to give Chris a hug. The difference between cleaning a roasting pan that has been wrapped in tinfoil and one that was not wrapped is at least ten minutes of misery. As Chris mentioned earlier, it also has benefits for cooking. I love it when that happens.

Start with a clean kitchen

Before guests arrive, make sure that every possible dish that can be cleaned is washed and put away. Get rid of clutter so surfaces are clear, and be sure the garbage and recycling bins are empty. It is much easier to keep a clean kitchen clean than play catch-up with a dirty kitchen.

Make certain the dishwasher is empty

Is there anything more frustrating when you are ready to clean than opening the dishwasher only to find it is full of clean dishes? Yes. Finding it full of dirty dishes. These are two scenarios you definitely want to avoid. Make sure the dishwasher is cleared out and ready to accept the dirty dishes as they happen. Consider running an interim cycle after cocktails, which can then be quickly put away before the big clean.

Clean as you go

As much as we want to devote our full focus to our guests and holiday merriment, the cleanup can get progressively worse if you don't stay on top of it. Whenever someone heads out for a cocktail, makes a trip to the restroom, or takes a peek at the turkey, they should do their best to bring something dirty with them back to the kitchen. Almost always there is something that needs to be put aside for cleaning or tossed, whether it be empty glasses, a bowl of discarded shrimp tails, or a scrunched up cocktail napkin. Be sure that whatever is brought out ends up close to its final destination. Instead of putting beer bottles in the sink, put them straight into the recycling bin.

Use a large ice chest as a soaking station

Before guests arrive fill a large cooler or ice chest halfway with very hot water and some dish soap and place it somewhere that is accessible but out of sight, perhaps in the mudroom or a nook in the kitchen. Soak the pots and pans as you transfer food to platters. This way, you are keeping the sink free for other duty.

Create the right atmosphere

Music, music, and more music. It's time to think Big Chill. In our family, we refrain from listening to any Christmas music right up until the Thanksgiving cleanup. For that, our playlist includes the peppiest Christmas music we can find.

 Download our Thanksgiving Cleaning Playlist on Spotify.

Delegate

"Many hands make light work" was a favorite saying of my grandmother. She was right. Delegating a specific task to each person will provide order and make everything go much faster. Think about passing around a list of cleanup tasks in a jar for the picking. Are some of your guests better left out of the kitchen? Ask Aunt Betty and Uncle Jack to read a story to the little ones or collect the napkins from the table.

Provide aprons

Be sure to have plenty of aprons on hand so people don't ruin those beautiful Thanksgiving sweaters—what would they wear next year? Short on aprons?

Check out our website for some fun ones!

Create stations

To avoid chaos, assign various parts of the kitchen as stations. Obviously, the sink is the washing station, but where do you want the leftovers to be managed? Where should dishes be scraped?

Clean the dishes first that are going home with your guests

Did Aunt Clara bring her famous sweet potato mash in her favorite ceramic turkey urn? Clean that first, so it is not sitting out on your counter for weeks as you try to find the time to drop it off at her house. By the way, when I bring a dish to a party I usually pick up a pretty serving piece at TJ Maxx or Home Goods, and gift it to the host. This way, neither one of us has to worry about washing it right then. While I am on the subject, I do the same with flowers. While I love flowers, and I do appreciate the sentiment of someone bringing them to me, it can be very distracting for a hostess to stop everything, find a vase, and arrange the flowers. Vases are so inexpensive, and if you are like me, you probably already have a few (hundred) in your basement. Is it just me, or do they actually multiply? Arrange the flowers in advance, add a bit of water for the journey, and then all you or the hostess has to do is fill the vase with water. Even better, the vase will now live in her basement.

Prepare for leftovers

If you are sending guests home with a care package, be sure to have disposable plastic containers and zipper bags at the ready. If you have a buffet table, think about inviting your guests to choose and pack up some leftovers before you set out dessert. Provide the containers or bags and a marker to write their name. You can do the same after dessert, and they can add that to their stash in the fridge… which by now should have plenty of empty (if temporarily) shelf space.

Provide an incentive

Leave time to do something fun after the cleanup—perhaps a game, a movie, or an after-dinner drink. People tend to move a little faster if there is something to look forward to.

Don't be a martyr

Either recruit lots of help in the kitchen to get it done quickly, or just clear the dishes, stack them, put the perishables away, and then spend time enjoying your family and guests. You and the rest of your household can tackle the remaining cleanup when guests have left.

Index